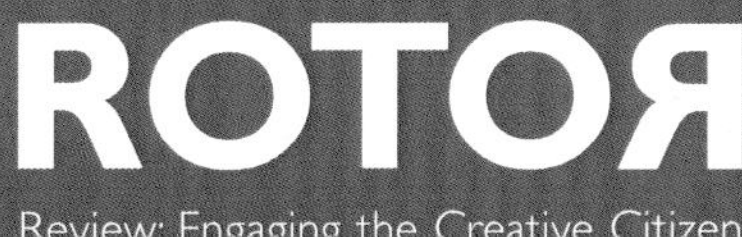

Review: Engaging the Creative Citizen

Preface

The ROTOЯ programme, launched in 2012, was a partnership between the University of Huddersfield and Huddersfield Art Gallery, funded by Arts Council England. Through four series of exhibitions and public engagement opportunities over a period of five years, the aim at its inception was to provide opportunities for engaging with art, design and architecture research outside of the University.

Delivered amidst a challenging landscape for the arts nationally and locally, and striving to utilise the town's cultural assets, ROTOЯ also sought to advocate for cultural democracy, asking, through its range of activities, how creative thinking and action might be nurtured and lead to the growth of places. In its second phase (ROTOЯ III & IV) ROTOЯ embraced an action-research approach (which gains insights from engaging in the activity itself), in order to ask how public engagement could more effectively be embedded into exhibition programming, marketing and interpretation for the programme.

ROTOЯ Review II is a sequel to ROTOЯ Review (published 2014) which reflected on ROTOЯ I & II. ROTOЯ Review II focuses on the second phase of the programme, ROTOЯ III & IV, which comprised five exhibitions at Huddersfield Art Gallery during 2014-2017, engaging a total of over 28,000 visitors.

The five exhibitions of ROTOЯ III & IV were: *Thought Positions in Sculpture, China East-West, Open House: A Collaboration of Experts, Migrations* and *Discursive Documents*. Some of these were curated by staff from the University, others by thoughtfully chosen partners from beyond the town who were engaging with the same research questions.

Some years have passed since the delivery of the exhibitions. From this critical and temporal distance it is easier to see how the ambitions, outcomes, insights and impacts of ROTOЯ III & IV aligned with the strategic planning of the University of Huddersfield. It sought transdisciplinary and collaborative solutions to some of the challenges facing humanity, forming strategic regional partnerships with policy makers and 'facing outward' rather than exclusively inwards to academic networks within disciplinary boundaries. Moreover, the programme corresponded to the mission of the School of Art, Design and Architecture to articulate complex relationships, promote creativity and engage communities.

The intervening years have also provided an opportunity to identify and reflect on how the research insights of ROTOЯ have continued to make an impact in Huddersfield. In 2018, the University launched a new cultural partnership with Kirklees Council. Temporary Contemporary extends the provocations and builds on the insights of ROTOЯ by holding exhibitions in the public realm rather than a traditional art gallery context. Temporary Contemporary has generated new insights into the value of mixed ecologies and place-based making. These insights continue to enhance the cultural offer of Huddersfield and facilitate access to visual art for people of the town and beyond.

We extend our grateful thanks to the five contributors to this publication, as well as to Huddersfield Art Gallery, Kirklees Council, all collaborators and contributors to the ROTOЯ programme, the audiences, Arts Council England and the town of Huddersfield.

It is in the spirit of cultural critique, transdisciplinarity and partnership that underpins both ROTOЯ and Temporary Contemporary that I am delighted to share with you a series of critical writings that form part of the legacy of the ROTOЯ exhibition programme.

Professor Donal Fitzpatrick
Art & Communication
University of Huddersfield

Introduction

ROTOЯ was a programme of art and design exhibitions, public engagement events, and related research, developed by the School of Art, Design and Architecture at the University of Huddersfield, in partnership with Huddersfield Art Gallery and funded by Arts Council England.

This publication presents the sequel to the first iteration of ROTOЯ Review (2014), which presented a range of reflections on the exhibitions comprising ROTOЯ I & II through some well-known and respected voices. Like the previous Review publication, this publication primarily offers an overview and celebration of the exhibitions, this time reflecting on the second phase of the ROTOЯ programme (ROTOЯ III & IV). Illuminated through the writings of a select group of individuals who provide insights into their experiences of ROTOЯ, the exhibitions are considered through a diversity of voices, with the further aim of reflecting the programme's broad reach in terms of the diverse audiences it sought to engage. In this introduction we also aim to communicate the broader context in which this second phase of the programme functioned. In addition to reflecting on the programme's evolution over the past seven years, it looks forward; exploring the early legacy of ROTOЯ and the evolution of the collaborations which underpinned it – not least its crucial partnership with Kirklees Council.

ROTOЯ I & II (2012-14) was conceived as a programme of 'Transdisciplinary Dialogue and Debate.' This notion encapsulated dual aims to explore different branches of knowledge production through art and design, and to focus on ways to engage audiences. ROTOЯ III & IV combined the initial aims of the ROTOЯ initiative with lessons learned from the earlier iterations and reflections on the wider cultural and political environment in which the programme was functioning in 2015-17. The programme of austerity bought in by a Tory government in 2010 had been steadily eroding funding and infrastructure for arts, culture and education. After 2013 this was joined by uncertainty and even anxiety about the UK's position in the world after then Prime Minister David Cameron promised an in/out referendum on membership of the European Union. Whilst ROTOЯ was not overtly political, the circumstances affecting culture in Huddersfield underpinned its thinking and development. The ROTOЯ III & IV programme was subtitled 'Engaging the Creative Citizen', positioning audiences at the centre of the broader cultural context.

ROTOЯ III & IV continued to think about providing opportunities for new audiences to engage with practice-based research spanning multiple disciplines. The next step on its logical journey was to situate the ROTOЯ model within the wider cultural vision locally, based around an ethos of cultural democracy, and securing for the programme some form of sustained impact and legacy beyond its period of Arts Council Funding. All of these aspirations were contained within its continued sense of responsibility for working to effect change, and to support new developments and thinking within art and design practices, cultural policies, and urban and economic strategies, encompassed by the belief that a long-term commitment to place-making, socially engaged practice and working in a creative, responsive manner brings about stronger communities that are more connected and mobile. With these overarching aims in mind, it was important for the programme team that ROTOЯ III & IV would expand on its existing stakeholder pool, nurture existing and develop new collaborations and, through both of these methods, seek to advocate for future programmes which might use a similar model to ROTOЯ; a model which places public engagement, collaboration, co-production and action-research central to its processes and philosophy.

The five exhibitions underpinning ROTOЯ III & IV reflected a diversity of disciplines, practices and curatorial strategies, and formed the nucleus of a much wider set of activities and events that constituted the programme. As part of its multi-layered engagement strategy, for example, ROTOЯ III & IV embarked upon an innovative and fruitful collaboration with Turvey World Dance, establishing a series of workshops and performances which ran in parallel with each exhibition. These sought to approach exhibition interpretation in a multi-sensory and non-prescriptive manner, with a view to overcoming some of the barriers to understanding and enjoying contemporary visual culture. Other engagement techniques which signalled a development from ROTOЯ I & II included the implementation of what might be considered '360 degree' engagement, whereby visitors were encouraged, during workshops and through the exhibition's creative feedback mechanisms, to enter into dialogue with the artists and with other visitors, to propose to the artists the sorts of questions they wished to ask of them; effectively holding a mirror up to its curatorial, exhibitionary and art-viewing processes. For the *Open House* exhibition, in the spirit of co-production fundamental to its conceptual identity, visitors were invited to collaborate with the artists and with the work, participating in the creation of exhibition content through ongoing opportunities for interaction and dialogue. Surpassing ROTOЯ I & II in terms of audience figures, engaging a total of 28,149 visitors to its exhibitions (an average of 74 per day) and over 5000 participants in its accompanying events and activities, was an achievement heightened by the challenging circumstances within which it was operating.

Image courtesy of Jamie Collier

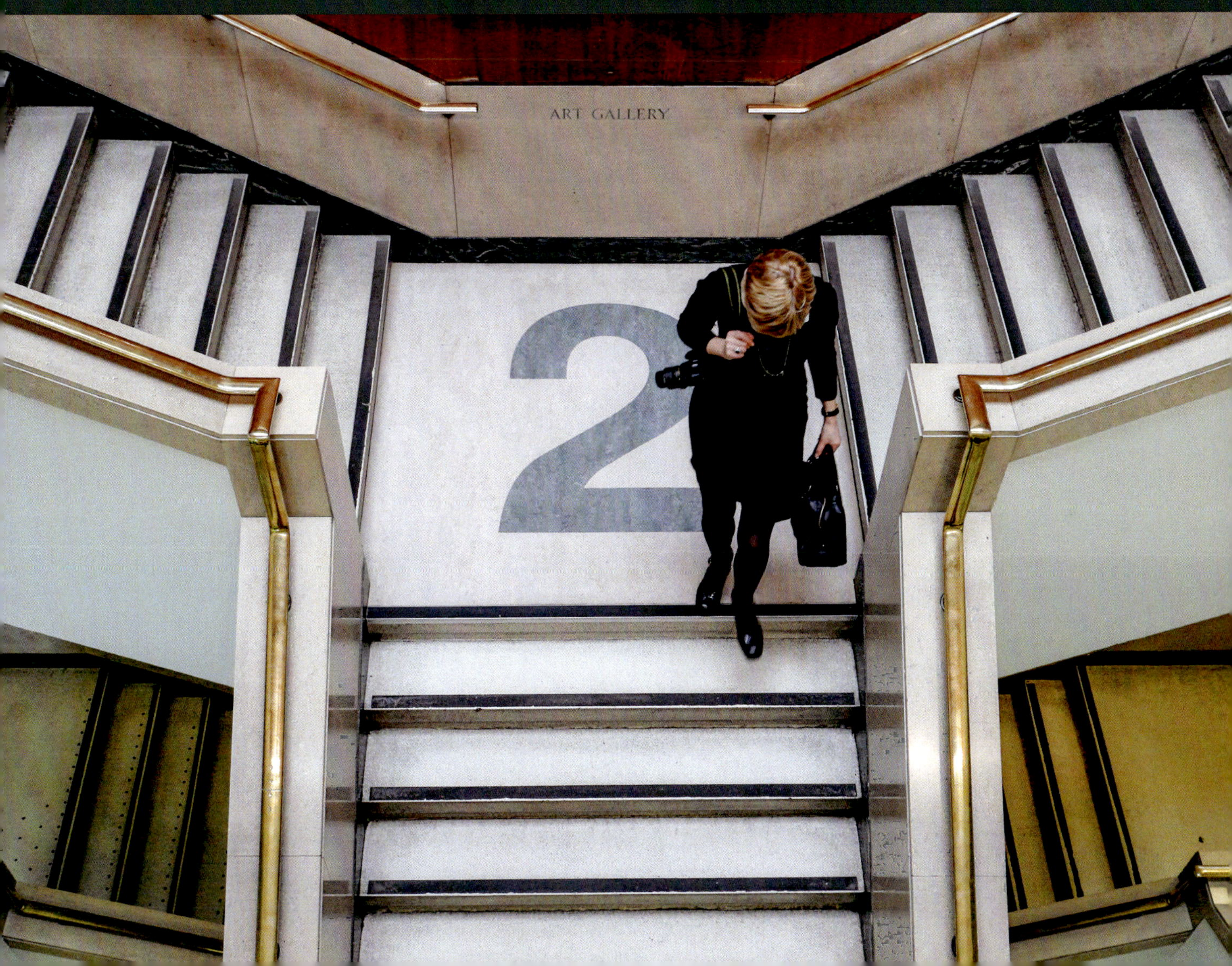

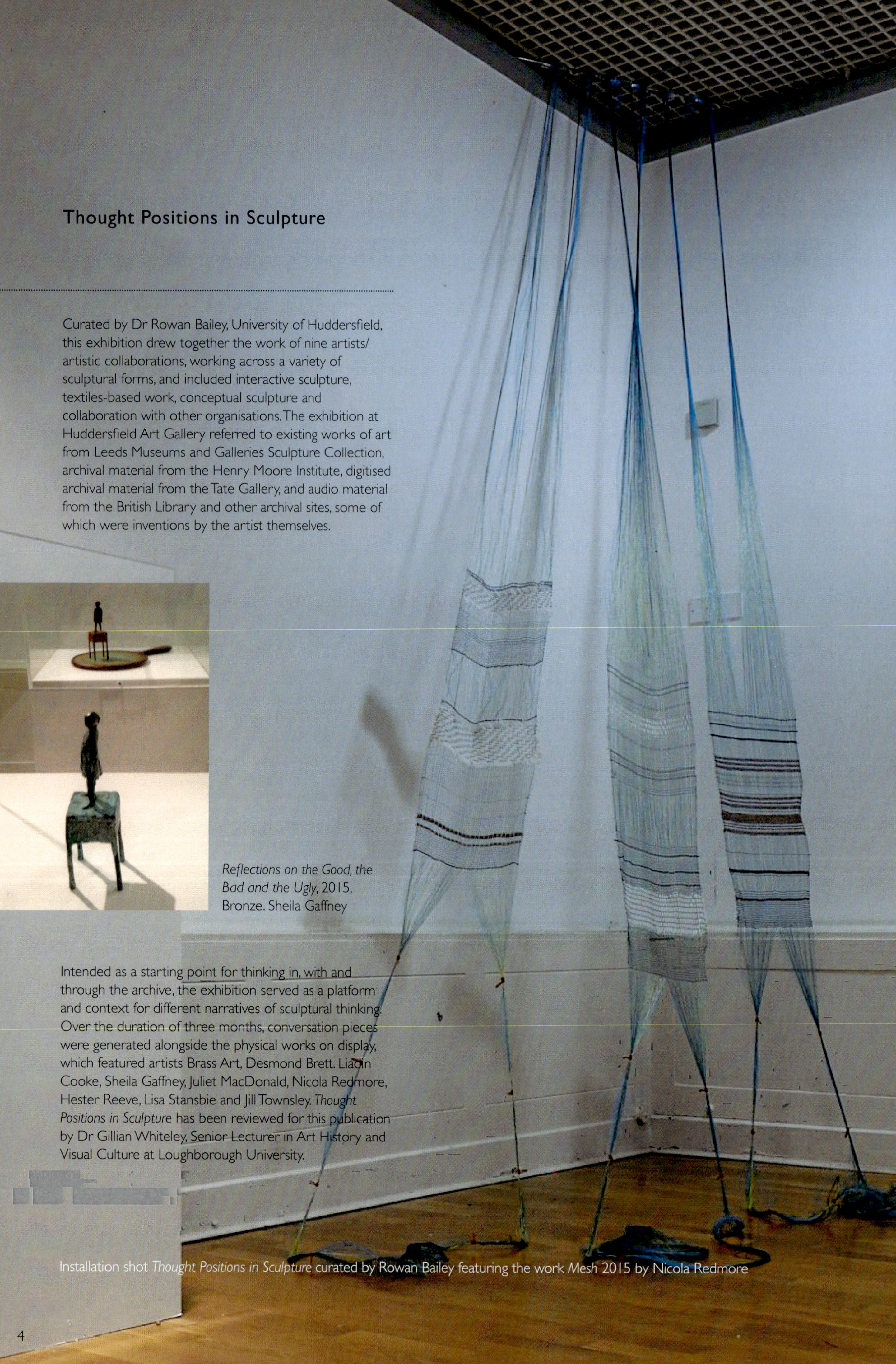

Thought Positions in Sculpture

Curated by Dr Rowan Bailey, University of Huddersfield, this exhibition drew together the work of nine artists/ artistic collaborations, working across a variety of sculptural forms, and included interactive sculpture, textiles-based work, conceptual sculpture and collaboration with other organisations. The exhibition at Huddersfield Art Gallery referred to existing works of art from Leeds Museums and Galleries Sculpture Collection, archival material from the Henry Moore Institute, digitised archival material from the Tate Gallery, and audio material from the British Library and other archival sites, some of which were inventions by the artist themselves.

Reflections on the Good, the Bad and the Ugly, 2015, Bronze. Sheila Gaffney

Intended as a starting point for thinking in, with and through the archive, the exhibition served as a platform and context for different narratives of sculptural thinking. Over the duration of three months, conversation pieces were generated alongside the physical works on display, which featured artists Brass Art, Desmond Brett. Liadin Cooke, Sheila Gaffney, Juliet MacDonald, Nicola Redmore, Hester Reeve, Lisa Stansbie and Jill Townsley. *Thought Positions in Sculpture* has been reviewed for this publication by Dr Gillian Whiteley, Senior Lecturer in Art History and Visual Culture at Loughborough University.

Installation shot *Thought Positions in Sculpture* curated by Rowan Bailey featuring the work *Mesh* 2015 by Nicola Redmore

China East-West: The Alternative Face of Globalisation in Urban and Rural Transformations

Curated by Professor Nicholas Temple, Dr Yun Gao and Dr Ioanni Delsante, colleagues in the architecture faculty at University of Huddersfield, this exhibition provided a 'window' into the dramatic changes taking place in Chinese urban and rural life. Exploring urban design in China through photographs, drawings, architectural models, maps and films, this architectural exhibition explored the changing face of regional urbanism and posed questions about how the environmental, economic and social challenges facing many parts of the world might provide opportunities for regional cities and towns in the North of England to develop alternative forms of urban living, which are fundamentally different from those of the rapidly expanding metropolises. It featured student as well as staff research, and students from both MA and undergraduate architecture courses were involved in supporting its engagement activities. *China East-West* has been reviewed by Luigi Stenardo, Associate Professor of Civil, Environmental and Architectural Engineering at Università di Padova, Italy.

Installation shot *China East-West* curated by Professor Nicholas Temple, Dr Yun Gao and Dr Ioanni Delsante

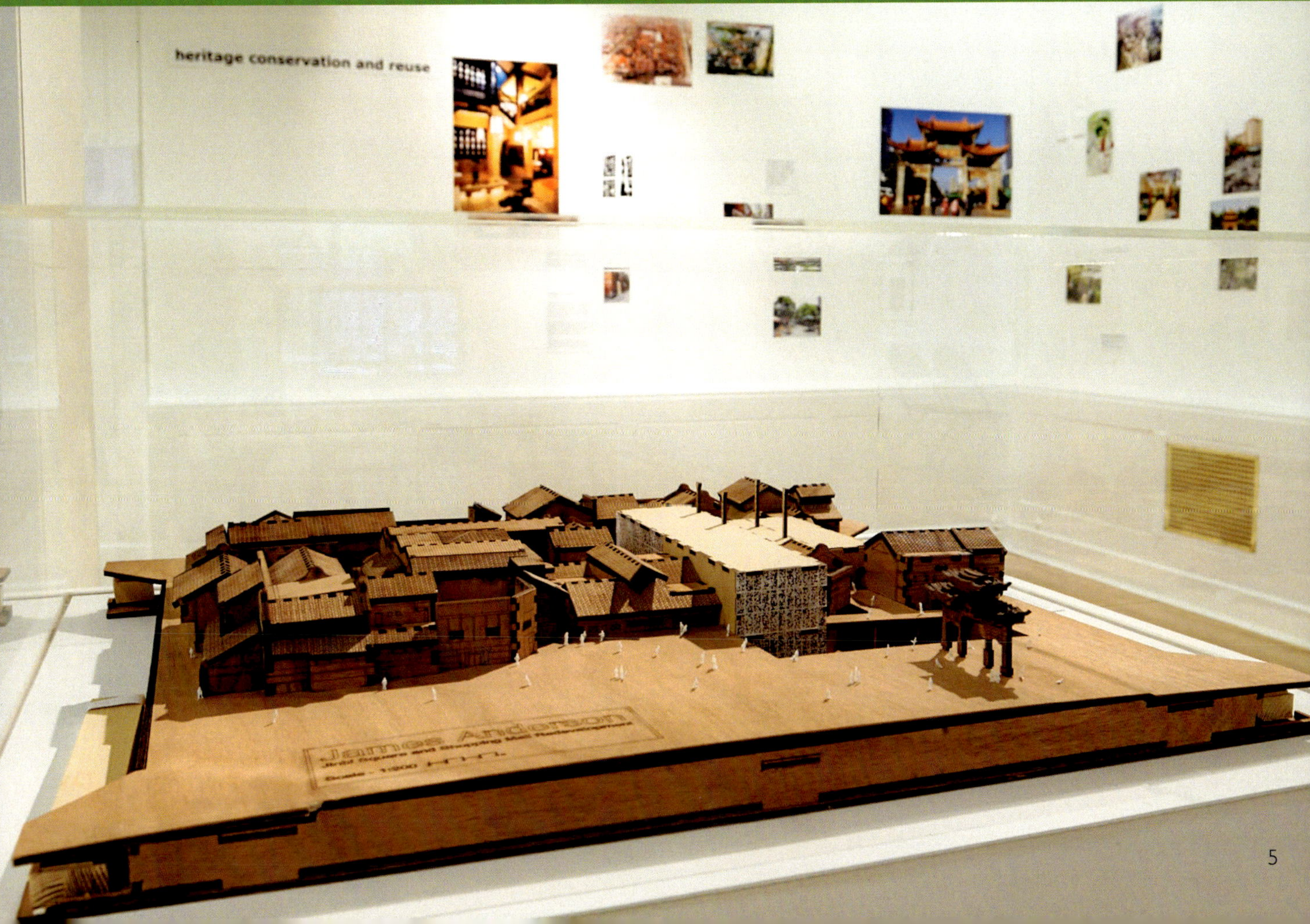

Open House: A Collaboration of Experts

Curated by Lydia Catterall, this exhibition signalled a new partnership between ROTOЯ and Leeds-based East Street Arts. It embedded public engagement at its heart through opportunities for interaction, working in a responsive manner to feedback as it was received, and focusing on Huddersfield and its people, as both a rich archive and motif to initiate a co-produced public exhibition. Remaining true to the 'transdisciplinary dialogue and debate' ethos that ran through ROTOЯ, the exhibition incorporated public workshops and artist residencies, forming a vibrant, open working space in which discussion was able to develop. It invited proposals from regional artists interested in working with local people, places and archives to respond, through exhibition content, to ideas around site, memory and community.

The selected artists – David Armes, Jim Bond, Liz Walker, Rozi Fuller, ReetSo and Nicola Golightly – had access to space within Huddersfield Art Gallery, which they used as their primary studio space during an initial four-week residency period. At the start of this four-week residency period, a 'skeletal' exhibition from the existing Huddersfield Art Gallery and Kirklees museum archives and collections, selected by each artist via early conversations with their community and with Gallery staff, formed an initial backdrop to the opening of the exhibition and acted at a starting point for conversations with visitors, which, in turn, fed into the production of new works of art. For this publication, *Open House* was reviewed by artist Gemma Lacey.

Installation shot *Open House: A Collaboration of Experts* exhibition curated by Lydia Catterall featuring the work of David Armes

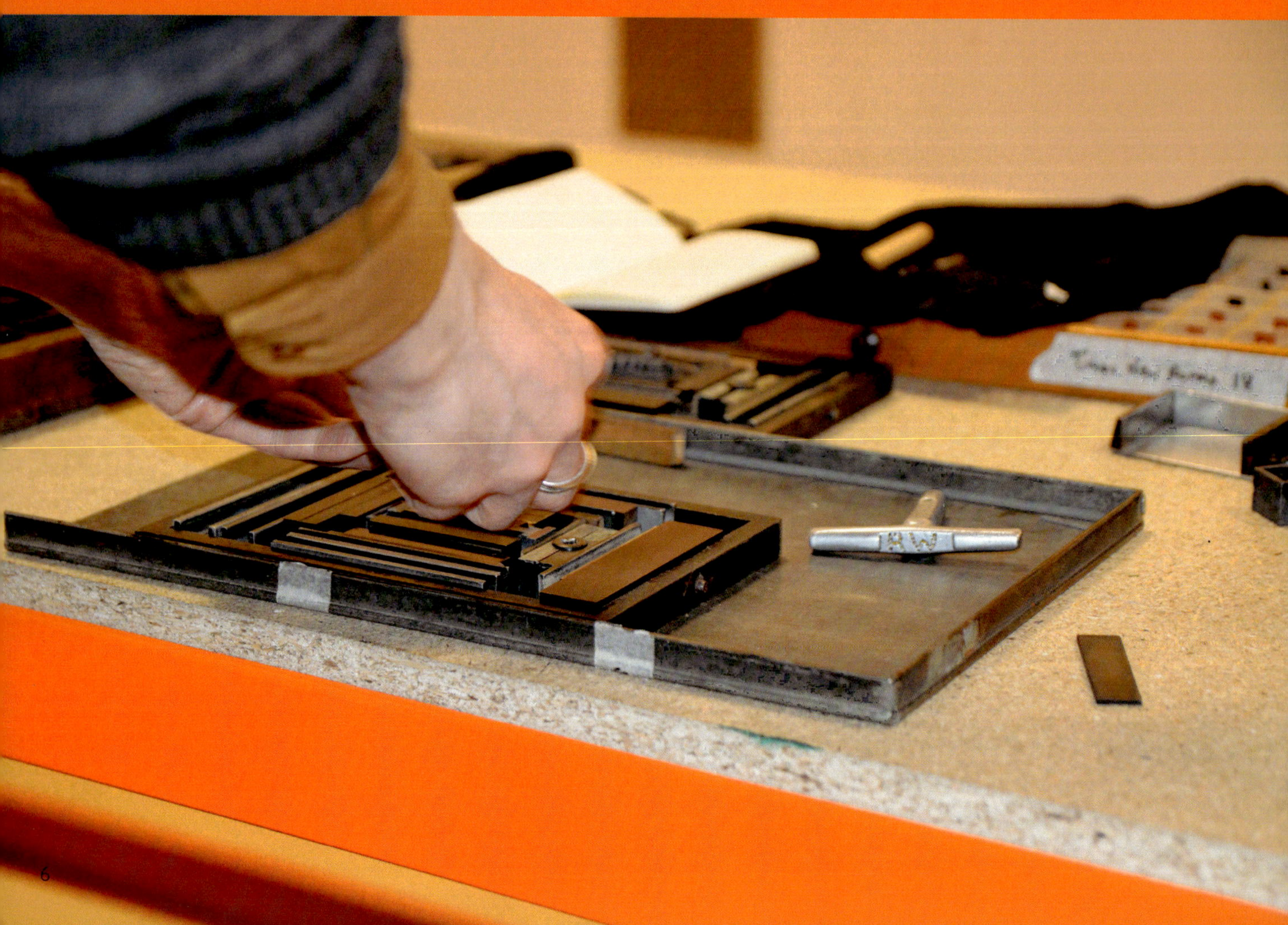

Migrations

Curated by Professor Jessica Hemmings, now of University of Gothenburg, Sweden, *Migrations* explored the notion of textiles as carriers of multiple cultural influences put forth in the accompanying publication, Cultural Threads: transnational textiles today[1], *Migrations* examined the ways in which cloth and fabric can act as cultural markers, their portability meaning that they will often travel with people around the globe. The exhibition also addressed the hybrid position of textiles within the worlds of craft, design and art. It featured as part of an international tour which included America, Ireland and Australia. The ROTOЯ exhibition made connections with Huddersfield's rich textiles heritage and Yorkshire's Year of the Textile, and it incorporated poetry-in-residence as well as targeted outreach workshops with local schools through collaboration with The Children's Art School, in addition to artist and curator talks, interactive, tactile interpretation methods, and Turvey World dance workshops and performances. *Migrations* was reviewed for this publication by Dr Christine Checinska, Associate Research Fellow at the University of Johannesburg and writer, designer, curator and dancer, who writes about textiles, culture and race.

Toril Johannessen, *Unlearning Optical Illusions I-IV*, 2014-18
Printed textiles

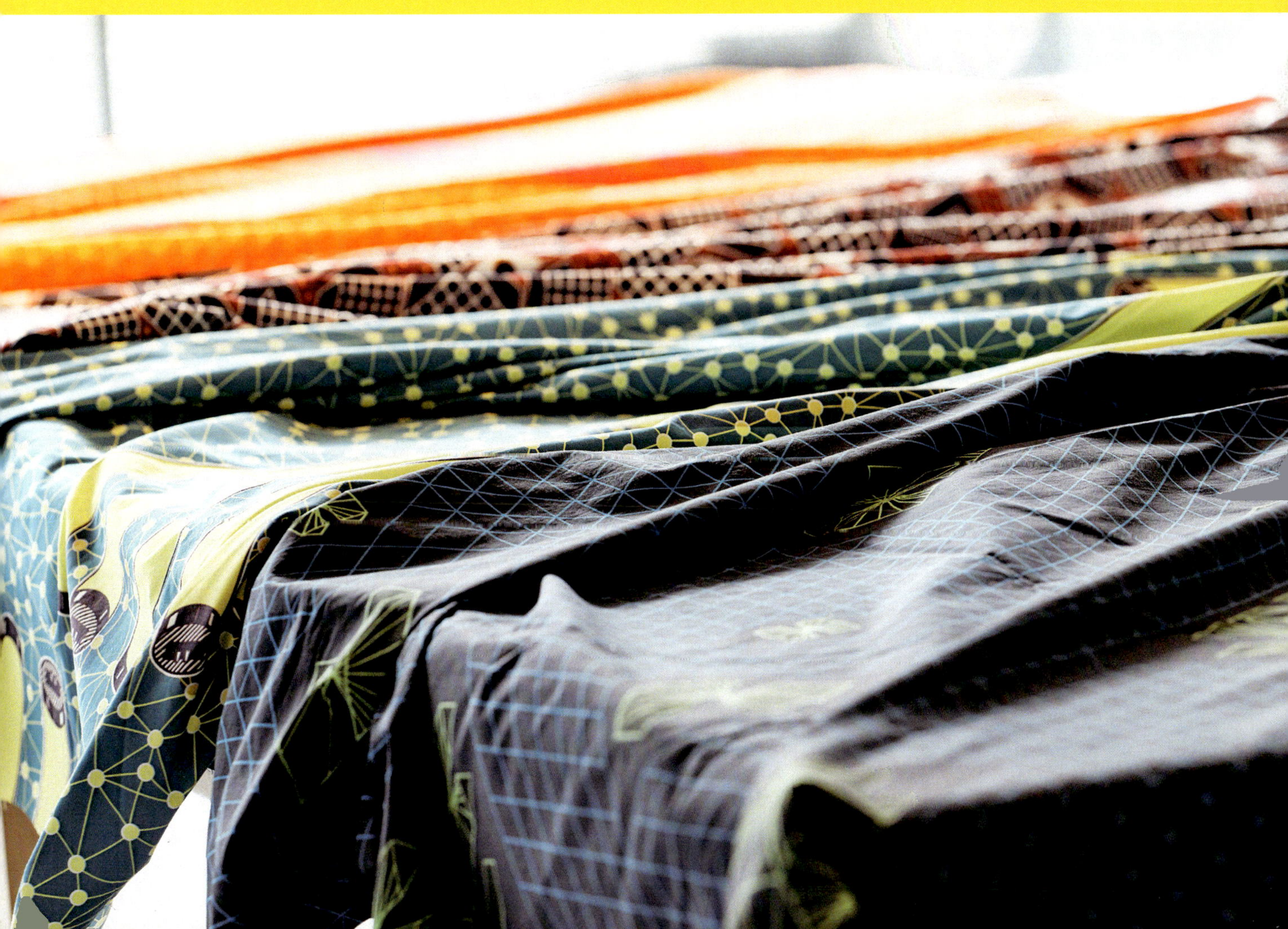

Discursive Documents

Curated by Dr Liam Devlin, University of Huddersfield, *Discursive Documents* further expanded on the dialogic element of ROTOЯ and its desire to communicate and connect effectively with its publics. It did so by exploring the photograph's potential to prompt debate, not necessarily to address 'how things are' but to ask 'what is possible'. It looked at how photographs act as both a document (of events or moments) and as an artistic/aesthetic image. Featuring the work of several key photographers, the exhibition addressed themes including migration and the body and invited visitors to situate themselves between the images to consider, question and debate the themes they explored; becoming a part of the dialogue between them. The exhibitions paired artists and photographers whose work could be linked thematically. Seba Kurtis's seductive and fragile images from Calais were set in relation to Alex Beldea's portraits and appropriated images from refugees fleeing the conflict in the Middle East. The everyday assumptions that we bring to photographs when we 'read' or try to understand them are challenged by both Richard Mulhearn and Richard Higginbottom's deliberately ambiguous images. Mulhearn's images celebrate those moments when we subconsciously slip out of the conventional behaviour expected of us; while Higginbottom's work is a response to cultural theorist Michel De Certeau's exploration of the complexity of the modern city, which he described as a 'swarming mass of innumerable singularities' (de Certeau 1984: 97). Finally, Layla Sailor and Sarah Eyre's work used collages and gifs to disrupt the flow of clichéd images of female bodies, and to explore the boundaries between objects and bodies. *Discursive Documents* was reviewed for this publication by Anna Taylor, artist and editor of *Backburner Journal*.

Layla Sailor, *Dolores II*, 2017
Digital Duraclear Print. Image courtesy of Silvana Trevale

Satellite exhibitions and projects

As part of ROTOЯ's commitment to making its exhibitions relevant and interesting to a varied audience, a further satellite exhibition was developed in collaboration with the School of Education and curator Olaojo Aiyegbayo. The exhibition showcased a series of historical British political newspaper cartoons depicting issues relating to race and ethnicity from the 1950s to early 2000s. Satirising racism, discrimination and immigration – issues with significant contemporary resonance – the exhibition was held across two sites within the University campus and enabled a new generation of students, staff and members of the public to experience the ways in which political satire can stimulate positive conversations around the importance of making equality, diversity and sanctuary a fundamental part of British culture.

A series of fringe events and activities supported ROTOЯ III & IV's continuing commitment to making all forms of art and design accessible, relatable and interesting to as many people as possible, while also aiming to communicate widely the ethos and ideas which underpinned the programme. These included events outside of conventional gallery spaces, such as a pop-up exhibition and young people's workshop in Leeds for its Unity Day festival, collaborations with the Children's Art School, Holmfirth[2], and workshops at the 2017 Engage Conference, Bristol. The latter acted primarily as a means of disseminating a newly developed toolkit – a collaboration between ROTOЯ and Fun Palaces who are an ongoing campaign for cultural democracy[3] . The toolkit, which was piloted at the conference, was designed as a free, downloadable resource to support those wishing to work collaboratively to develop public-facing arts events and activities, by prompting questions, suggesting possibilities acting as an ice-breaker tool for groups working together for the first time. Positively received at the conference, it presented ROTOЯ as an exemplar and model for ways of exploring the provision of cost-effective cultural services within a locale.

Image courtesy of Silvana Trevale

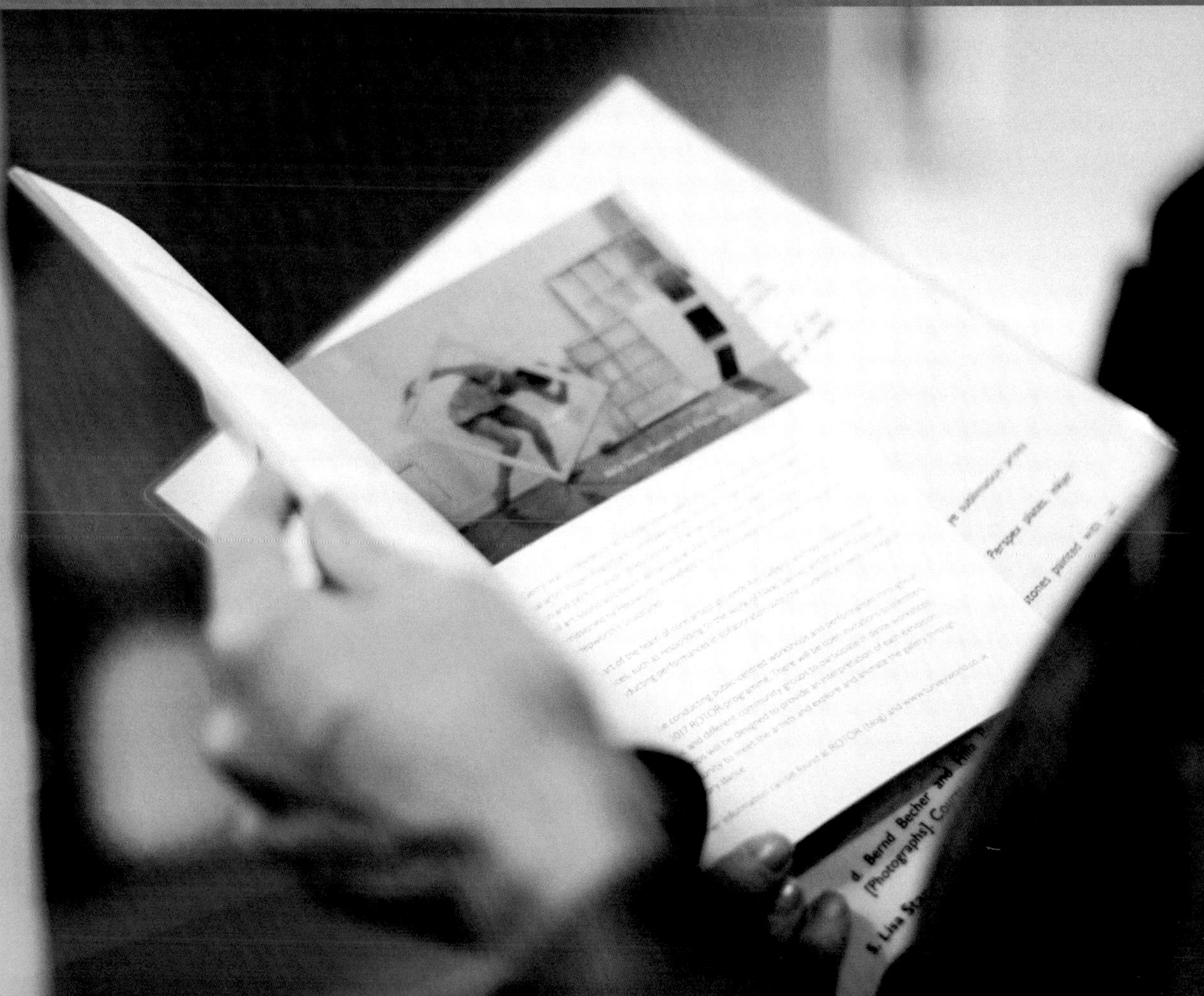

Presenting the insights of ROTOЯ

ROTOЯ III & IV expanded its scope in a research context, working in a cross-disciplinary manner to connect with other research projects happening across the University. It had a presence at the 2017 Researchers' Night at the University, which saw young people from across the UK exploring the programme and participating in activities that sought to broaden understanding of, and share learning from the programme. ROTOЯ further inaugurated its own evolution as a form of action-research, in which its approaches to exhibition design and delivery acted as a self-reflexive mechanism for assimilating learning back into the programme, as well as communicating it externally. The effect of this was a responsive programme in which cumulative changes were trialled around its engagement, interpretation, marketing and dissemination methods as each exhibition progressed.

Marking the culmination of the two phases of ROTOЯ and its 13 exhibitions, and to continue dialogue and learning around the ways in which partnership working and cultural leadership might be used to reinterpret and rejuvenate a place's cultural offer, a ROTOЯ conference entitled Culture, Community, Creativity was held in January 2018 at the Lawrence Batley theatre in Huddersfield. As well as disseminating and celebrating the programme's outcomes, the conference also positioned our goal of exploring new challenges and possibilities for an art and design programme in the region. The speakers, panelists and workshop facilitators at Culture, Community, Creativity were invited from a range of backgrounds and from across a breadth of specialisms, and included academics, professionals and individuals representing organisations, from across the arts and cultural sector both in the UK and internationally.

The questions and provocations which underpinned Culture, Community, Creativity and which were opened up to participants for further discussion were those to which ROTOЯ had aimed to respond through its exhibitions and events, and those which emerged from the programme, at times as unexpected outcomes. They were recognised, through having worked with a range of stakeholders, as being transferable to a breadth of projects, practitioners, organisations and institutions both locally and further afield. ROTOЯ, then, was positioned simply as the starting point or catalyst for what was a series of engaging discussions around the challenges and benefits of projects which aim to achieve one of ROTOЯ's key visions – of exploring how we create the conditions for creative thinking and action to flourish. These discussions had an emphasis on the intersections of the arts, people and places, and asked participants

Installation shot *Open House: A Collaborative of Experts* exhibition curated by Lydia Catterall featuring an outcome from the ReetSo public workshop.

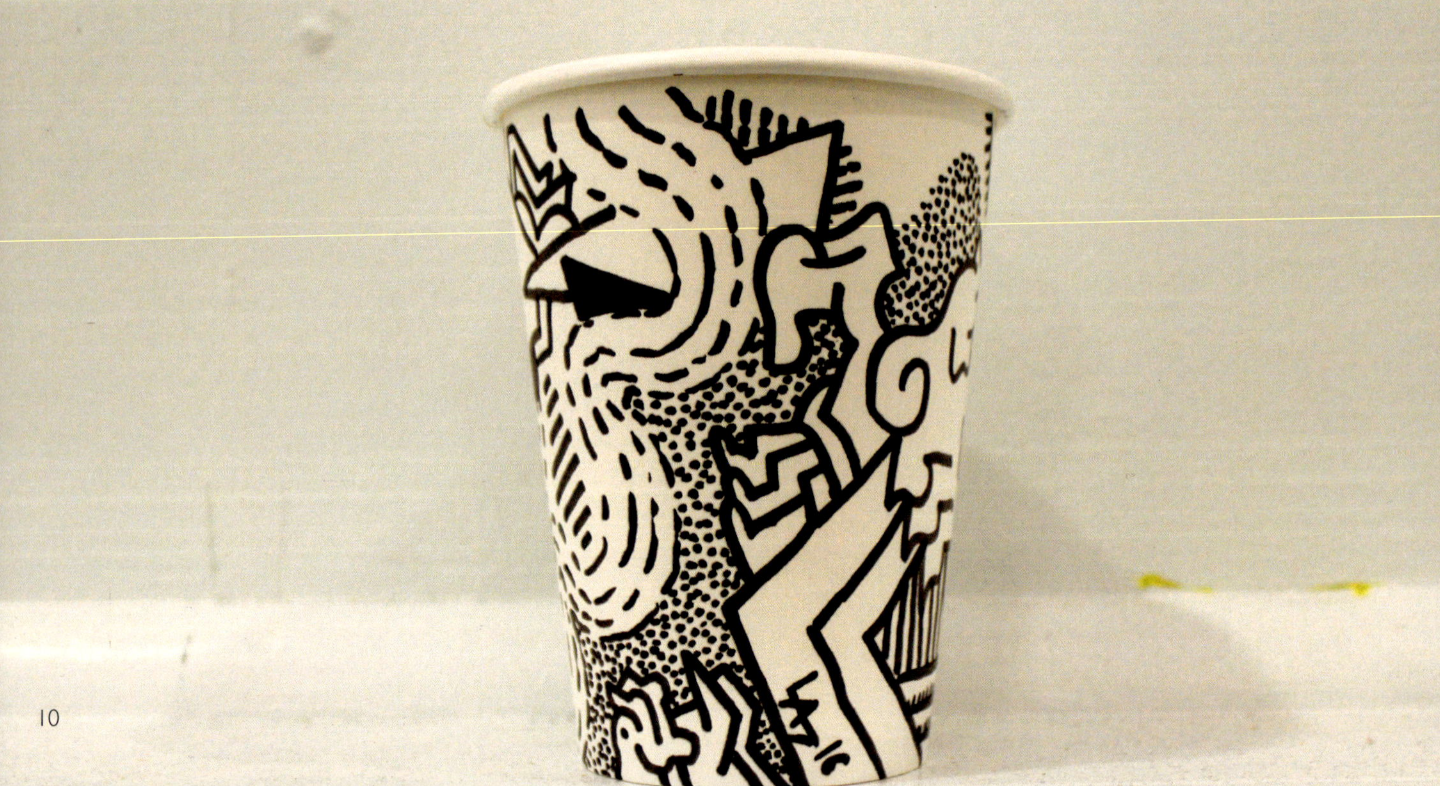

to consider the significance of cultural democracy in our contemporary context. It addressed the role of partnerships and collaborations in helping to nurture the cultural offer of an area, and explored the ways in which cultural organisations and services can successfully reflect on the creativity and aspirations of the people who use them. Specifically, it asked:

- How might creative thinking and action be nurtured and lead to growth of places?
- What is the role of the arts in place-making?
- How can businesses, universities and cultural organisations support 'peripheral' artistic activity and is this the correct term to use?
- How do we support the economic and emotional resilience of artistic activity within towns and cities?
- In what ways can artistic activity enhance a sense of citizenship, ownership and belonging?
- How might DIY or fringe activities and opportunities function as cultural animators of a place?
- What do we mean by 'cultural democracy' in the context of local arts initiatives?
- How can effective cultural advocacy be implemented to ensure that arts projects are less a temporary intervention and more a long-term vision for a place?

Reflecting this conference retrospectively, it can be considered a 'bridge' between ROTOЯ and the development of Temporary Contemporary, a partnership project between Kirklees Council and the School of Art, Design and Architecture at the University of Huddersfield. Temporary Contemporary's aims expand on many of the concerns addressed by ROTOЯ around place-based making and collaboration. Temporary Contemporary had increased emphasis on the ways in which an exhibition and events programme might utilise action-research to become a test bed for exploring creative production and situated curatorial practice, and for prompting conversations about cultural and mixed ecologies – the ways in which different artistic and non-artistic disciplines develop and negotiate with each other. The first year of the Temporary Contemporary programme was situated in Grade II listed retail destination Queensgate Market, with contributions from university lecturers, artists, local artisan producers, musicians, students and young people. It continues to act as a catalyst for cultural production in Huddersfield.

Dr. Anna Powell
Senior Lecturer Art and Design Theory
University of Huddersfield

Dr. Linda Jean Pittwood
Research Assistant Art and Visual Culture
University of Huddersfield

The editors gratefully acknowledge the enormous contribution to ROTOЯ of Professor Steve Swindells who taught in the School of Art, Design and Architecture from 1999 to 2017.

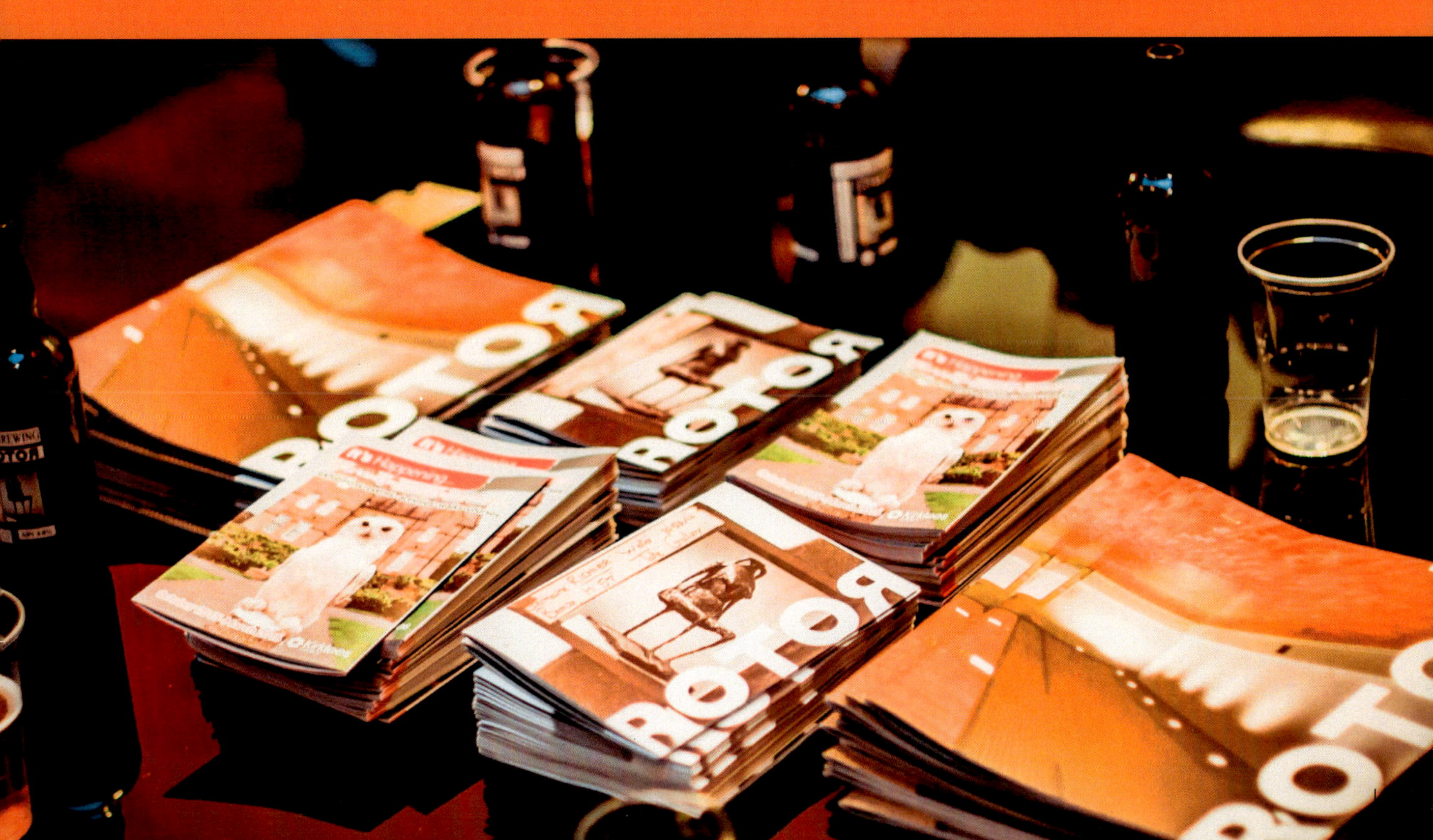

Subject(ive) positions. Thinking about thought positions in sculpture

First thoughts, subject(ive) positioning. In a former life, and in the pre-postindustrial pre-internet Seventies, I used to drive over to Huddersfield regularly through the bleak gritstone moorlands of Penistone, collecting paper cheques from grimy hands at various small but thriving manufacturing companies. Textiles, coal, steel, engineering, 'light' trades, 'heavy' trades: then, Yorkshire was noisy with the rhythms of workshops, mills and factories. I have crossed the Pennines many times since, occasionally catching improvisation gigs, safely ensconced in the avant-garde enclave of Huddersfield Contemporary Music Festival[4]. But now, on a cold dank mid-December Saturday, instead of sweeping down the valley from the M62, past the site of the former magnificent Gannex mill of Wilson's 'mac' fame[5], I rumble into Huddersfield by train. Exiting the railway station in driving rain, rivulets form on the concourse. I pause to admire the recently renovated splendour of the station and its adjacent civic architecture[6], but it quickly fades in the deluge. The downpour drenches the stonework, as the former wealth of the town ebbs away amongst the ubiquitous signifiers of cut-price outlets and charity shops.

Soaking wet now, tramping through the town centre to the pretentiously named Piazza Shopping Centre, a run of low-level Sixties retail units opposite the steps of the library building, flanked by James Woodford's sculptures representing the two 'spirits' of art and literature, and up to the top floor and the tranquility of the municipal gallery[7]. Alone, anticipating my thoughts, I sink into the leather sofas as rain taps on the roof windows. Across in another gallery space, two sodden bedraggled figures are huddled together, sitting quietly, staring, thinking. Are they tired, homeless, lost? I strain to hear their conversation, my thoughts straying from Laurel and Hardy to Vladimir and Estragon, Rosencrantz and Guildenstern, Charles and Franz. I move into the gallery housing *Thought Positions in Sculpture* and try to make sense of where I am and what I encounter.

Second thoughts, enigmatic thinking and sculpture.

> 'the fragile mark as filled frameworks without cultural precedent'[8]
>
> 'they functioned locally as separate from a miniature'[9]

The complex and multi-layered nature of the project is evident at the entrance to the space, where there is a cardboard box containing a pile of A3 posters which turn out to be a selection of 500 computer-generated 'poetic thought positions'[10]. Enigmatically, like Alice, I am invited to take one. I take two posters, ponder the incomprehensible quotes, and step inside as the puzzle starts to unravel, revealing the exhibition itself as a starting point for a labyrinthine set of connections between things and ideas across a range of platforms that, over time and further investigation, makes for a rich experience. In a single gallery, the exhibition brings together a disparate array of objects, wall-based pieces, sculptures, installations, sound and video works. The curator, Rowan Bailey, invited nine artists to encounter and respond, in whatever way they chose, to documents, objects and materials in various archives, including the Leeds Museum and Galleries collections, papers in the archive collections at the Henry Moore Institute, digitised archive material in the Tate Gallery and audio material in the British Library. Initially, and to the casual visitor reliant on the exhibits themselves, it was quite tricky to work out what was going on as, in many cases, the inspiration for the artists' work was absent, forcing the viewer to imagine what precisely the works were responding to. That said, the artworks' detachment from their sources added a layer of obscurity, emphasising the whole experience as one which demanded a painstaking cerebral approach. Indeed, the exhibition itself initiated a discursive rather than affective or somatic encounter with things, objects and materials. This was enriched by the reflective narratives produced by each of the ten artists, the online 'conversation pieces', many of which were densely researched, which were posted serially over the course of the show.

The artworks generated a series of dialectical conversations within the exhibition space itself: materiality and immateriality, absence and presence, time and space. Consistent and incongruent temporalities emerged. Sheila Gaffney's contribution signalled a dialogue with the absent but familiar histories and discourses of twentieth-century sculpture, a 'thought' resonating with the work of postwar artists such as Ralph Brown, Reg Butler and, in this particular instance, Germaine Richier. Noting that her return to modelling represents an attempt to reclaim and legitimize her own 'symbolic capitol as a sculptor and change the history in figurative sculptor where men make feelings about women', she presented two tiny bronze figures, in her wittily titled *Reflections on the Good, the Bad and the Ugly* (2015). Gaffney's online 'reflections', poignantly and precisely, explore a life's journey working with the haptic and with a kind of sculptural consciousness[11]. Her references to Reg Butler's *Girl on a Round Base* (1968-72), take me back to my lengthy interviews with Rosemary Butler, a former student and later his partner within a set of complicated domestic relationships[12]. One day, we turned off the tape and she took me through his studio, no longer the male domain but now populated with Rosemary's work, to the garden

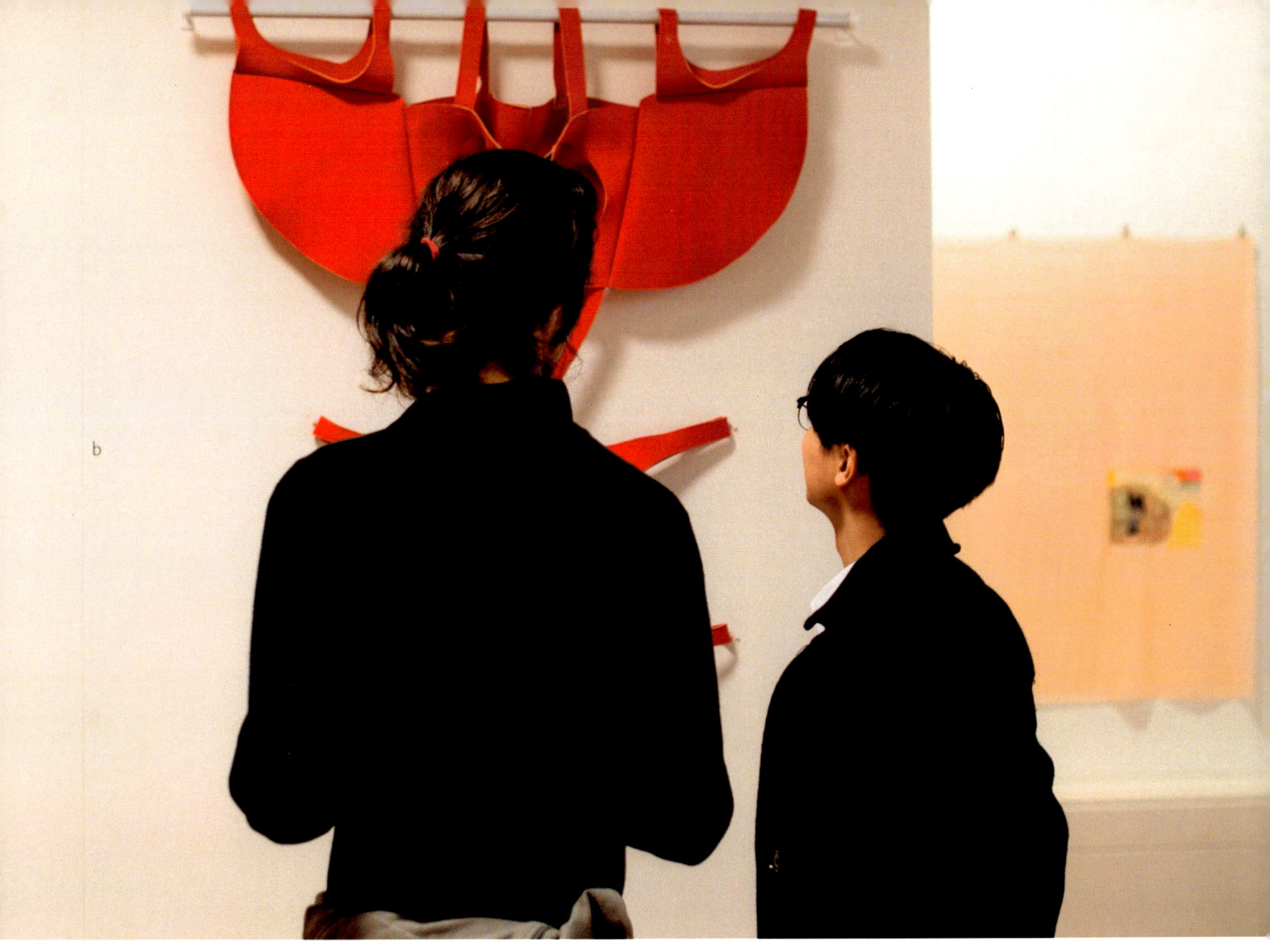

Installation shot *Thought Positions in Sculpture* exhibition curated by Rowan Bailey featuring *Swimming Costume*, 2015, Lisa Stansbie.

shed where she pulled the plastic sealed wraps from a pile of dusty objects, revealing the body parts of Reg's life-like painted bronze 'girls', their 'shame' hidden from view in the dark recesses. I found their faux verisimilitude both alarming and sad. Gaffney's artistic and textual responses highlight a range of complex issues that spring from an embodied subject(ive) positioning in relation to sculptural 'value', calling attention to the need to constantly re-view and re-think our interpretations and responses to artworks in different contexts and at different times.

With other exhibits, the spatial and aesthetic relationships of the 'parasite' artworks to their 'hosts' was interesting; sometimes the relationship was close and affirmative, paying *homage*, whereas in other pairings the umbilical cord was more ambiguous or detached. Sometimes the offspring resisted, it fought back. Some artworks were exhibited alongside their 'hosts': Nicola Redmore's woven piece, *Mesh* (2015), hugged a corner near two of Kenneth Armitage's pink plaster maquettes from 1951. For me, Jill Townsley's installation of 'archives' – her meticulously polished stones, nail varnish bottles and dyed plates inspired by a series of the Bechers' *Pitheads* (c.1957-1975) also on display – provided a rich taxonomy of hue and materiality. It worked with, around and beyond the Bechers' obsessive printed images. Like the river-bed to which it alluded, Townsley's work had an ecology all of its own, opening up a multi-faceted conversation with discourses around the natural and the synthetic.

Working with an aesthetic of fragility, Juliet MacDonald's *Desert Victory* (2015) also functioned on many levels, projecting the ghostly traces of film footage from the Imperial War Museum onto the roof of the gallery, installed alongside bronze fragments, Henry Charles Fehr's precious *Head of Victory* (1922) and the artist's small experimental drawings. Viewed alongside a reading of the artist's essay, in which she referred to her fascination with the 'frailties and fissures of the figure of Victory' that reminded her of a 'holographic image'[13], the combined piece provided a richly researched visual and critical dialogue around the glorification and loss of war.

Other pieces in the exhibition demanded deeper thinking to solve the puzzle of connections. Hester Reeve's sculptural installation, *Burning to speak* (2015), had detached itself from its 'host' and was fighting back, refuting the biographical material - in this case, paradoxically, the British Library National Life Stories Artists' Lives audio archives, some of which I had contributed to more than a decade ago[14] - that had initiated the work. As she wrote,

> instead of prioritising the voiced content, I strained my ears for the reverberation of larynxes that had been inked with a non-linguistic thinking-ness. By this I mean a human being's muscular aptitude for being shaped by life as opposed to the habit of assuming one is a container enclosing a tiny part of it.[15]

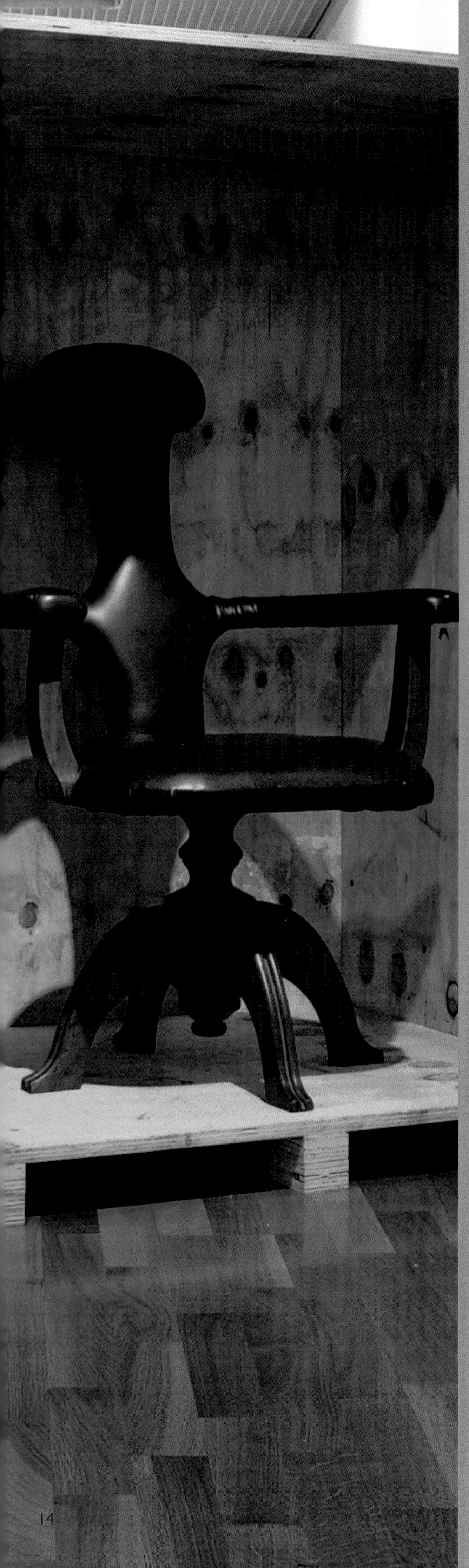

contraption in the gallery, revealed an assemblage of roughly chalked aphorisms. Every one held a provocative or nonsensical thought that reverberated back onto the questions about 'sculptural thinking' at the heart of this project.

Final thoughts, repositioning. The ROTOЯ programme sets itself a number of tasks including, as it declares, the generation of dialogue and debate and through its activities and exhibitions that not only speak to the gallery's existing audience but reach out to new audiences. This particular ROTOЯ project set itself an ambitious task: the curatorial aim was for the archive to provide a starting point for 'different narratives of sculptural thinking'. And it did all this in myriad ways and reaching out across a range of platforms, in the gallery space at Huddersfield and into the twittersphere beyond, engendering a multi-layered and multi-sited provocation for thought. For me, the project also engaged with a set of current critical and philosophical understandings and debates about thought and materiality. Maybe the two guys huddled together in the other gallery space weren't just waiting for the rain to stop but were deeply engaged in sculptural discussion and thinking.

Thought Positions in Sculpture
10 October 2015 - 9 January 2016

Curated by Dr Rowan Bailey
Director of Post Graduate Studies, Art, Design and Architecture, University of Huddersfield

Reviewed by Dr Gillian Whiteley
Senior Lecturer in Art History and Visual Culture
University of Loughborough

Detail of Sigmund Freud's study chair [replica], as part of Brass Art, *Freud's House: the Double* (2015) Audio video installation: looped video (4:5 ratio), packing crates, replica chair courtesy of the Freud Museum, London. Binaural sound created by Monty Adkins with Brass Art. Programming Spencer Roberts.

China East-West: The Alternative Face of Globalization in Urban and Rural Transformations

The *China East-West* exhibition showcases differences, as well as similarities, in the urbanisation and urban transformation processes in China. By selecting two relevant case studies, Shanghai and Kunming, the exhibition provides striking evidence of the tumultuous and uneven changes across the country, with its East/West divide. The curators have organised the exhibition across two broad areas of investigation meant to be shared by such different contexts: urban and rural development, and heritage, conservation and re-use. As such, it provides two parallel narratives based on case studies illustrated via drawings, photos, models, films and interviews with designers.

In terms of urban and rural development, the exhibition showcase at the very beginning the initiative of Shanghainese new towns (such as Pujiang, Anting and Thames New Town), included in the broader 1-9-6-6 strategy (1 central city, 9 new cities, 60 new towns, 600 villages). The video "Urbanisation in China; happiness is seen everywhere" by David Lingerak (D-FILM), together with the reflections offered by Harry Den Hartog (2010)[16], offer an astonishing, although not totally unexpected, view on rapid urbanisation that links to matter of sustainability, community engagement, gentrification as well as social inequalities. As such, there are other case studies that explore these dynamics in other places: the sustainable urbanisation process of Chongming island including upgrading and retrofitting existing settlements (by Chen Yi[17]), or the rural villages such as Qinkou and Zixi in Kunming area. Moreover, within the context of rapid urbanisation new architectural topics are emerging. Tong Ming, for example, explores the concept of architectural typology as an opposition to banalization and homologation in sprawl town and suburban areas.

The second section focuses on urban and architectural heritage, its conservation and reuse. It showcases creative districts in Shanghai, including the forerunner case study of Xintiandi: a mix of conservation and development, heritage and urban regeneration approaches. More recent case studies are the so called '1933', a former slaughterhouse, and the Power Station of Art, a Shanghainese contemporary art museum which was refurbished as part of the Expo 2010 masterplan, the equivalent of the Tate Modern, which occupies the former

Installation shot *China East-West* curated by Professor Nicholas Temple, Dr Yun Gao and Dr Ioanni Delsante featuring dancers from Turvey World Dance. Image courtesy of Roger Boygott

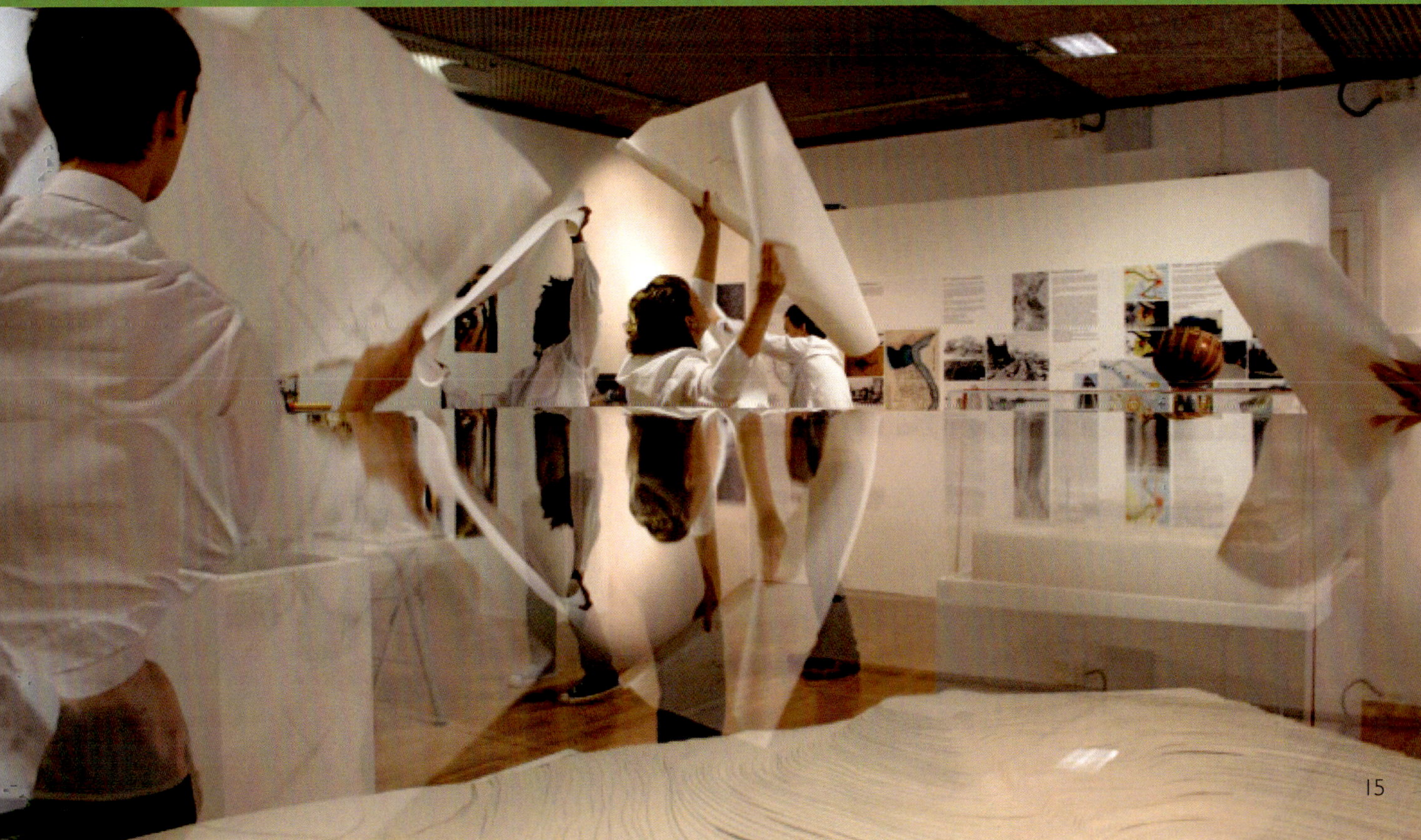

Bankside Power Station in London, UK. Moreover, the exhibition highlights Tian Zi Fan neighbourhood, where the government acknowledged the local community aspirations against the process of urban transformation. Even if tourism and consumption-based activities facilitate gentrification processes and have almost completely substituted art production and hand crafts, Tian Zi Fan provides opportunities for further investigating the means of the Creative City as well as community engagement and empowerment.

Sustainability, given its potential ambiguity and multiple significance, has not been identified in one area but it underpins various projects from different perspectives. It manifests related to the environment and rapid urbanisation, and elsewhere relates to the social and cultural sustainability of rural villages and heritage preservation. It is interesting to note how the concept is variously interpreted by Chinese architects. Wang Shu, Pritzker Prize in 2012, makes reference to the reuse of waste materials, but also to traditional construction techniques and the visual evocation of historical walls. Philippe Yuan develops his own atelier via the 'Silk Wall' project. The building, part of a creative district, is fully refurbished by using a mix of low and high tech. Low tech in the use of materials, but high tech in design.

Projects are enriched by a number of videos, including some interviews with Chinese designers and scholars. Several large models complement the visual apparatus and provide an insight into specific design practices and three-dimensional thinking.

The exhibition represents the outcome of a variety of activities, including field work, interviews and on-going research projects in between the curatorial team and a number of Chinese universities. It shows the potential to further develop research activities: for example on rural villages and their communities, as well as on the role of spatial practices in art based urban transformation projects. Interestingly, some of the challenges seem to be shared in between different areas of China, despite the huge differences and uneven development in between Shanghai metropolitan region and Yunnan inner area. The East/West divide symbolised by the case studies calls for innovative methodologies, based on multi-disciplinary and interdisciplinary approaches.

China East-West: The Alternative Face of Globalization in Urban and Rural Transformations
30 January - 23 April 2016

Curated by Professor Nicholas Temple, Dr Ioanni Delsante & Dr Yun Gao, Architecture, University of Huddersfield

Reviewed by Professor Luigi Stendardo, Università di Padova, Italy

Installation shot *China East-West* curated by Professor Nicholas Temple, Dr Yun Gao and Dr Ioanni Delsante.

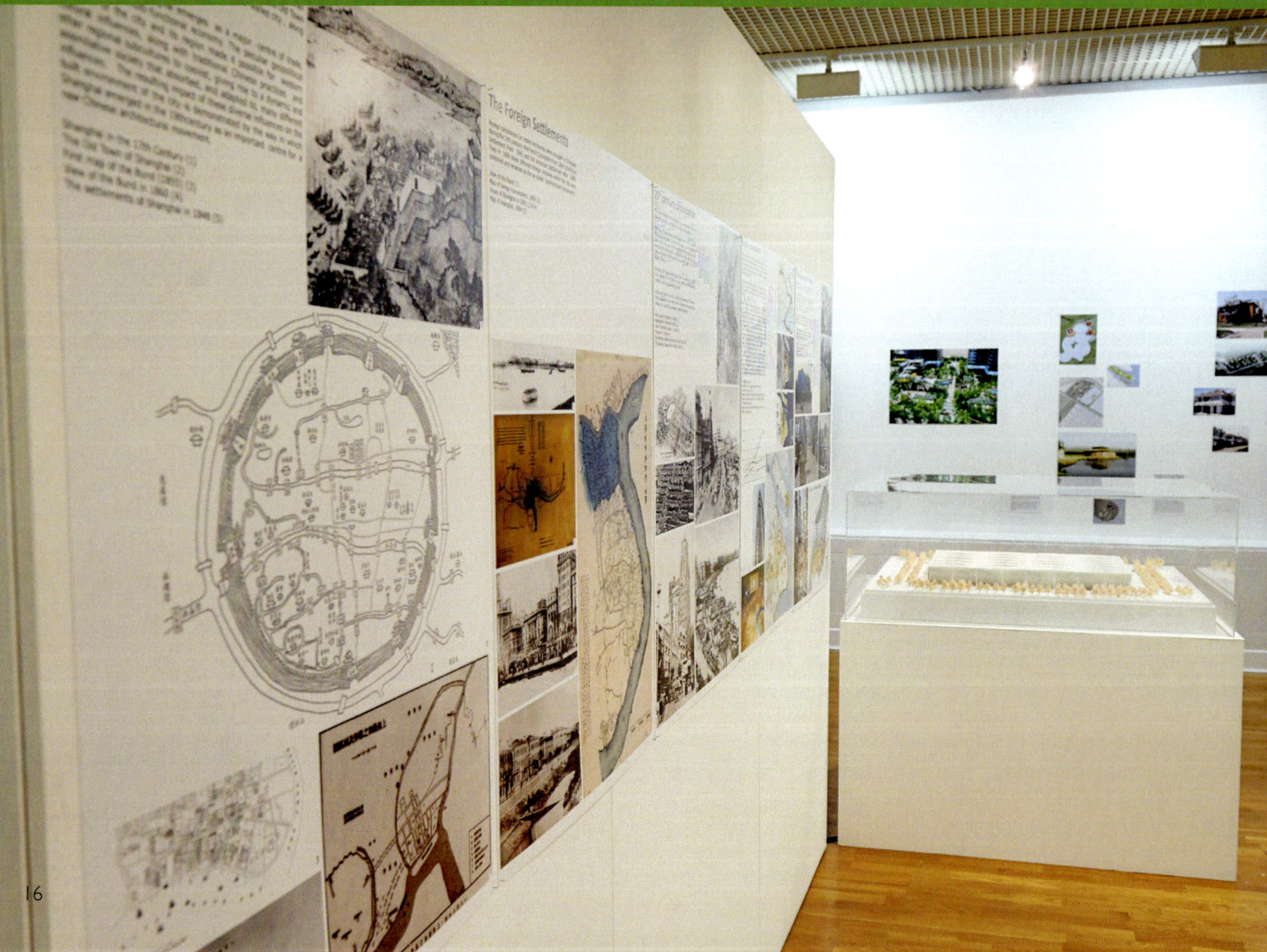

Open House: A Collaboration of Experts

Huddersfield Art Gallery as subject, studio, engagement and presentation space. Two project briefs running concurrently in adjoining rooms. Huddersfield under inquiry - its history and sense of place as held in the town's collections and memories.

Preview

Arriving at the gallery for the first time, reassured by its 1930's sturdy symmetrical design. The quiet broken over cheese-tasting notes and bread-making tips, appetite and interest piqued. A brief dance piece improvised in response, provides pointers, a way in to the exhibition. Like the dancers are starting a conversation, 'I think this' except it is more 'I feel this'. A physical response unmediated by language opens the space for consideration.

Archives: a response to the archive collection - Jim Bond, Liz Walker, Rozi Fuller

A series of cloth-wrapped umbrellas hang on the wall, looking like cocoons. Their muslin bags made especially for them, labels tied about their necks.

Fragments of paper, maybe portions of patterns, pegged to a line, hold the shape of a lung or a continent. A4 sheets of text are pegged nearby.

Installation shot *Open House: A Collaboration of Experts* exhibition curated by Lydia Catterall featuring the work of David Armes.

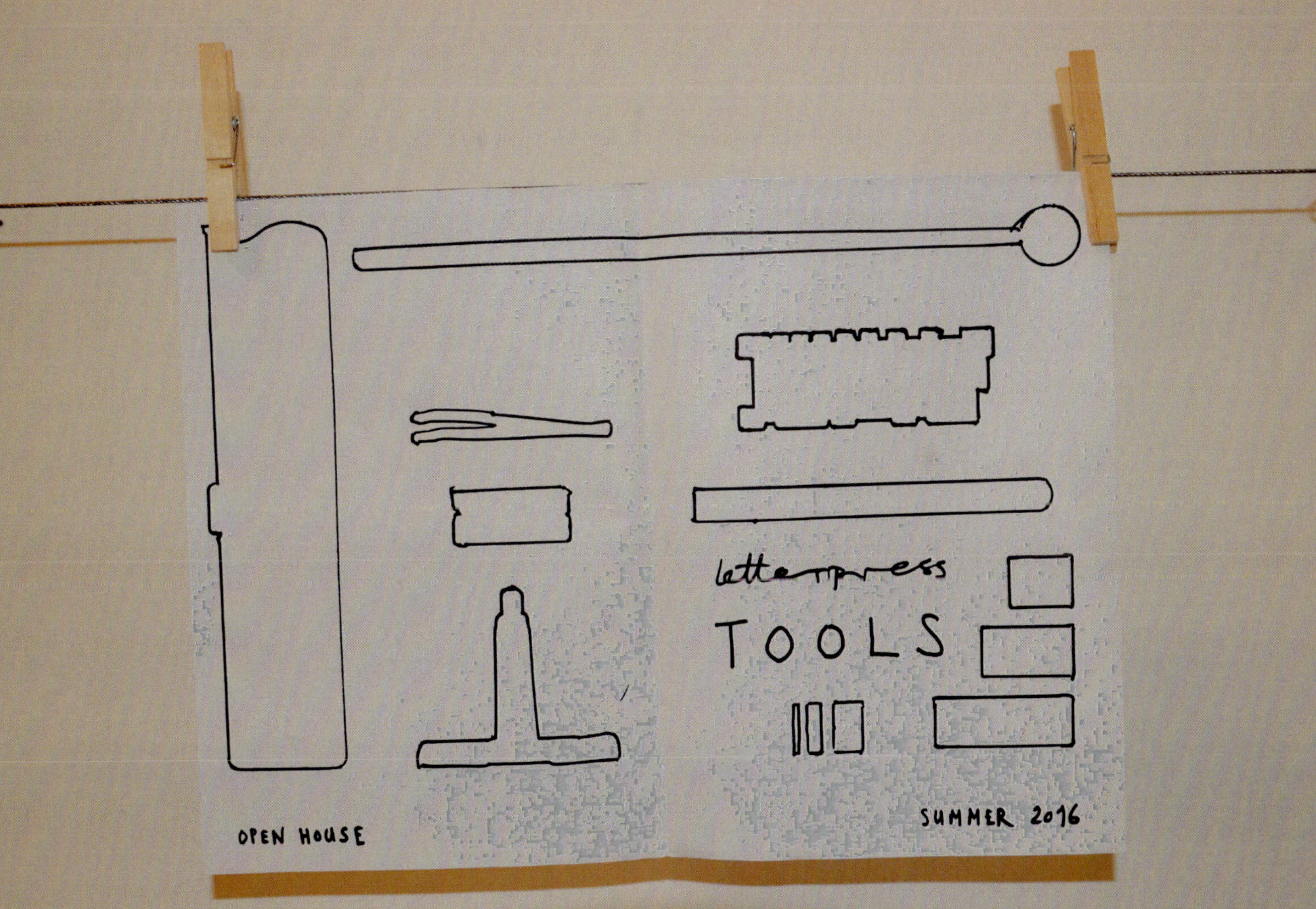

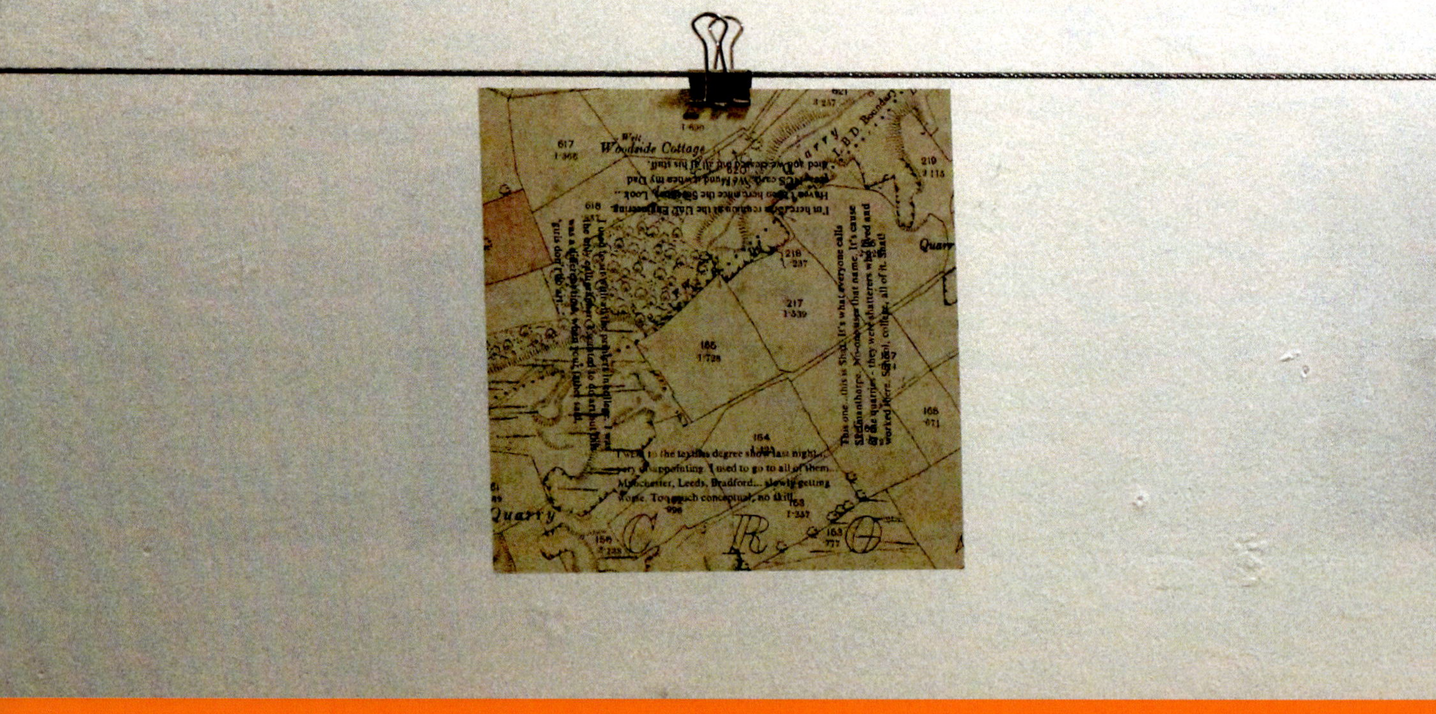

Installation shot *Open House: A Collaboration of Experts* exhibition curated by Lydia Catterall featuring the work of David Armes

A barrier; wooden posts and string erected between audience and display. Guiding us through the space. A loose ending that can be traversed. Is this barrier part health and safety, part work, part presentation?

The floor demarcated by lemon yellow tape, forms a grid through which boundaries are established; objects can be referenced or studied further.

A stuffed dog, alert on a plinth, looks up to the corner of the room. A tattered label hangs loosely down between its front legs.

A mannequin, blank calico canvas, stands to the side, upright; neck, no shoulders, tight puffed-up chest, nipped-in waist. 'S' bend hips stop just short of the bottom curve.

A bakelite doll in a glass vitrine sits upright surrounded by slices of things trapped in slides and glass jars, spot-lit.

A typewriter waits with an open invitation to type, to catalogue memories.

The space is low lit, intimate, controlled. There is a sense of drama and tension in the gallery held in the potential life of these objects. Their patina - rusted, worn down and dusty - sets a window into a world.

A counter-weight attached to a work table provides a rhythm to the looking and sorting as it moves down and up with the ticking clock to shine a light on the scene set for the short animation projected onto a metal mesh panel.

Behind the miniature desk the gentleman, spindly like the umbrellas, sits and considers objects. Wraps them, types their labels, hangs them up on pegs with care. Does the same to himself. The film ends, the counter-weight swings the light back; we are left with the objects.

Wayfinding: an exploration of the Art Gallery in Huddersfield - David Armes

A working space defined again by lemon yellow. The tape creating a block to walk around, this time there is no barrier, you can move as you like. The balanced grid of the floor echoes the building's design and location in Huddersfield. The town planner grid repeats in the work through blocks and units. Map squares hang on a line along a wall just ahead of their repeating shadows, creating a tile and tessellation when you follow.

Separate units patched together create something like a textile. The edges and corners of the patches bend and curve in towards themselves creating texture on top of the text printed on them. Tissue paper prints hang in front of light boxes, sighing as you pass by.

On the central block three Adana hand presses sit in line, ready for production. Their handles and disks at rest but set at such angles they look ready for action. The repetition of their form creates movement in the still space, like a set of trumpets in a modernist painting.

A film plays on a small screen. A man, close up and at a distance, feeds a scroll of paper through the hand presses, pushing down on the handles one at a time, carefully feeding the scroll through. His repeated movements, once in the gallery space, now fill the frame of the screen.

A sense of purpose in a well-lit working space. A gallery animated by a sifting and making process represented through repeated action and form. The thoughts of others sought out and triggered by this activity are documented, layering up on the surfaces of the room.

A long, light scroll of paper traces the form of the gallery. Running along its ledges and over the door frames. The length holds the phrases picked up, set and printed during

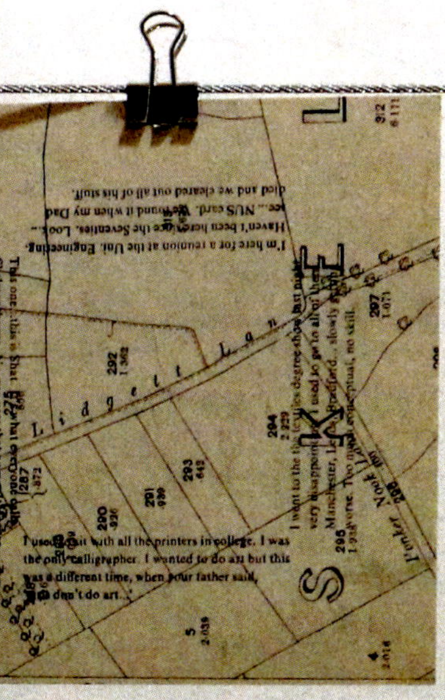

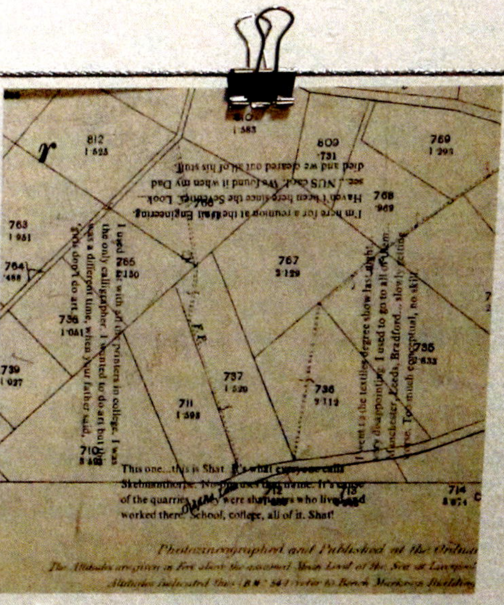

the residency: directions to the gallery, snippets of memory, recollections of Huddersfield, anecdotes and thoughts evoked. Recollected in the detached space of the gallery, the memories and phrases become directions anew.

Workshop - Gerry Turvey

Another viewing, with maybe ten others from the community, some familiar, some unfamiliar with the gallery and dance. A look around with questions posed. 'Respond in movement; to this piece, this idea, to each other'. Dialogue initiated. Challenges faced. Look, experience, respond, explore, respond, explore, look again. To consider elements of each space - responding to concept, composition, motion, noise, placement, colour, content - physically and emotionally. We align our breathing with the sigh of hung tissue paper. Knees and elbows imitate the jerk and bounce of the counterweight. We take cues from the gaze of the dog and the memories of others set into print. We play games; replicating the creative processes employed. Recalling our journeys, giving directions, moving to the directions of others. Using the grid format to shift around the space, we reflect upon ways around the town, navigating streets, pavements, steps and handrails whilst negotiating another's personal space and experience. Navigating their limbs and joints, finding a balance, an understanding, providing a support.

A finish of sorts

A large audience fills the gallery with limited movement and view. Behind the *Archive* barriers dancers shift in an opposite space to the public. They cosset and hold and consider each other. In *Wayfinding* they swap sides, move the audience about. They play the space, the objects displayed, some of the materials used and even, it seems, the people present. We witness the activation of the gallery. We jostle together, interact more openly, like familiars, for this brief time as the space is subverted, the held breath air of the gallery dispersed for a while.

Once the dance is done we return to the artwork energised and with new awareness. We search with our minds and our bodies, reflecting the movements of the dancers; to look from new angles at the quotes from previous visitors, to consider our breath in line with the hanging tissue, our reach up to the directions that frame the gallery doors and trace its cornicing. We consider the placing of ourselves in relation to the proportions of the space, its contents, the gallery building, the town of Huddersfield. We inquire within if we desire to be wrapped up in muslin and hung labelled on a peg for posterity, or to commit ourselves to some form of enquiry and documentation. Noting and caretaking in our lives and communities.

Open House: A Collaboration of Experts
28 May - 27 August 2016

Curated by Lydia Catterall, East Street Arts

Reviewed by Gemma Lacey

Migrations

Migrations, the international touring exhibition curated by Jessica Hemmings, took as its departure point the notion that multiple stories of cross-cultural exchange and post-colonial entanglements are embedded in textiles' folds, patterns and textures. The ease with which textiles can be worked, embellished, manipulated and transformed, then folded, packed and transported across the globe ensure that they are on the move just as people are on the move. Those forced to take flight carry few possessions, often travelling with literally the clothes on their backs[18]. Textiles become saturated with cultural meanings as they pass from person to person and continent to continent. Such is the power of textiles to carry varied and layered cultural references. Such is the potential power of textiles to 'speak'. In this show, Hemmings continued a conversation about the relationship between textiles, hybridity and the movement of peoples that began with the publication *Cultural Threads: Transnational Textiles Today* (Bloomsbury: 2015). Content sensitively gathered from contemporary artists, designers and writers, all using textiles to explore these themes, created a uniquely intimate, meditative and timely exhibit. The featured creative practitioners were Dan Halter, Pamela Johnson, Françoise Dupré, Toril Johannessen, Claire Barber, Mr Somebody & Mr Nobody, Godfried Donkor and Jasleen Kaur.

On entering the Huddersfield Art Gallery I was not only struck by the exuberance of colour displayed, but also by the gentle back-and-forth motion of cloth that had either been hung against the walls or from the ceiling in the case of London-based French-born artist Françoise Dupré's work. The work that in my view best captured the curator's concern with the movement of textiles and peoples was Zimbabwean Dan Halter's video piece *Space Invader (Johannesburg Taxi Rank – Port of Entry)*. Halter filmed aerial views of taxi ranks situated at policed border-crossings between Harare, Zimbabwe and Johannesburg, South Africa. Watching the video it soon becomes apparent that as well as witnessing the shuttling to-and-fro of migrants one witnesses the carrying here-and-there of distinctive inexpensive woven plastic shopping bags ubiquitous to cosmopolitan urban landscapes. These bags are seen in many places all over the world and are used in a variety of different ways – as luggage, for laundry, shopping or storage. Although the title of the work evokes the eponymous video game, Halter's video reminds us that stories of global mass migration mask individual stories of displacement, un-belonging and economic inequality. The plastic shopping bags could thus be seen as symbolising psychological baggage as well as carrying essential material goods. The use of the term 'invader' is all the more poignant in today's context where the threat of national borders being over-run by vast numbers of migrants and/or refugees is used to win political votes in Europe and the USA.

Françoise Dupré utilised similar plastic shopping bags collaged and stitched together to create characteristically brightly coloured hangings and sculptures. These bags were a familiar feature of the multi-cultural eighteenth arrondissement in Paris where she grew up. Hemmings explains that these bags are derogatively known as "Ghana-must-go bags" after the 1983 law that saw the deportation of illegal immigrants (often Ghanaian) from Nigeria. The recycled leftover carrier bag handles that are pieced together to form *Stripes* seemed to me to act as a metaphor for those whom society discards, like the expelled Ghanaian labourers.

Where Dan Halter used video to map the crossing of borders, British artist Claire Barber used 'ten journey' ferry tickets to trace the patterns created by the commuters on the Hythe Ferry. The punched holes in the spent tickets so closely resembled those found on dobby looms that Barber hand wove patterns onto their surfaces using unravelled threads drawn from the garments that she repeatedly wore whilst crossing from Hythe to Southampton during the making of *You Are The Journey (An Embroidered Intervention)*. This in my view is a reminder of the intimate nature of this media and the way in which we continually interact non-verbally as humans. The notion of multiple journeys taken over a period of time represented by Barber's strategically tangled threads also brought to the fore the notion of mapping personal and collective diasporic histories through textiles. This notion was exemplified by artist Godfried Donkor's work.

In the video piece *The Currency of Ntoma (Fabric)* Donkor turns his focus to his mother's collection of "Holland prints" also referred to "Dutch Wax prints". (Donkor is a Ghanain artist based in London) His mother traded Dutch Wax and therefore had a vast collection of fabrics. She is shown explaining the meaning and significance of each piece. Some fabric designs carry the names of proverbs. Some are named after political events of local and global importance to the region. Some express joy, some longing. The video footage of the artist's mother is interrupted by footage of a male figure, the Chief Dresser to the king of the Ashanti, swathing himself in twelve yards of heavy black cloth. The bulk of the cloth being worn reflects the status of the wearer. In the exhibition video Donkor explains that in making the work he was keen to explore the aesthetics of the men wearing the cloth and the theory behind the women collecting it. The

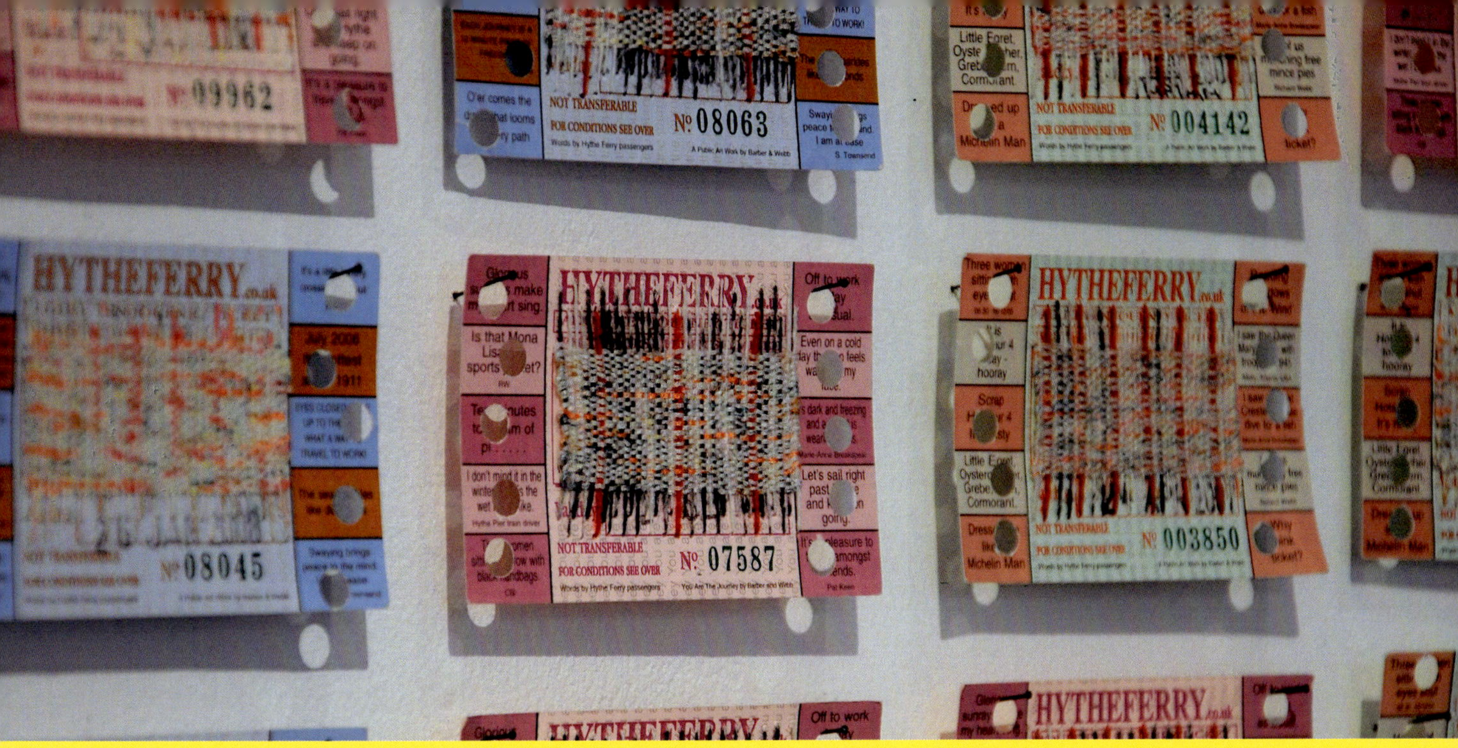

Detail of *You Are the Journey,* 2015 Claire Barber. Photography by Claire Barber

term 'currency' in the work's title refers to flow, to the idea of a stream and also to money. Dutch Wax could be seen as the ultimate transnational cloth having its roots/routes in Indonesian batik production, journeying to West Africa where the Dutch colonisors of Indonesia stopped to resupply, re-emerging in global capital cities such as London, Paris and New York. They have come to symbolise a fictitious, one-dimensional 'Africa'. Donkor's video challenges this association and flattening out of meaning. The physical and metaphorical unpacking of his mother's archive calls to mind the Ghanaian artist El Anatsui's observation that 'the scope of meaning associated with cloth is so wide…. [It] is to the African what monuments are to Westerners.'[19]

South African born artists Mr Somebody & Mr Nobody (Heidi Chisholm and Sharon Lombard), took up the East African textile tradition of the *khanga* or 'proverb cloth' to explore and challenge perceptions of African cultures. The two apply contemporary statements onto fine Indian cotton, printing in Cape Town using a silkscreen printing process, stitched in North Carolina and transported to Miami for distribution. By placing these reworked *khangas* into dialogue with Donkor's mother's '(hi)-story cloths', Hemmings subtly points to the easily made, yet oft mistaken, assumptions regarding the cultural specificity of certain textile craft techniques.

The geographical and historical roots/routes of Dutch Wax cloth also provided a starting point for Norwegian artist Toril Johannessen. Johannessen created digital prints based on the optical patterns found within Dutch Wax prints' batik effects. The viewer was invited to handle these textiles presented in billowing folds across a table set within view of Donkor's video. This satisfied my impulse to touch - an impulse that stems from the familiarity of textiles; they are after all part of our everyday lives. Textiles in a sense represent forms of embodied knowledge. Furthermore the haptic quality of textiles potentially closes the distance between the artist, curator and audience, allowing for multi-perspectival cross-cultural conversations.

The wrapping of a Sikh turban about the head of an Englishman in Scottish-Indian designer Jasleen Kaur's photographs was at first sight somewhat puzzling. Why is an elderly Anglo-Saxon man being made to wear a turban? Who are these people in these photographs? What is their relationship to one another? Kaur's photographs were taken during her *Dear Lord Napier* project (2010). They depict the artist and her father tying a turban onto the head of the current Lord Robert Napier, the significance being that his grandfather, Sir Robert Napier, played a pivotal role in the British annexation of the Punjab. In an initial correspondence to Lord Napier about his grandfather Kaur explained: 'he was a central figure to the story of British India … and someone who helped to open up the migratory relationship between India and Britain that enabled my Sikh great grandfather to come to Britain.' Kaur viewed the act of wrapping Lord Napier's head as a celebration of the 'dialogue between two communities of different cultures, languages and religions'[20]. Migration not only breeds loss, displacement and un-belonging, it also seeds new hybrid cultures, networks of layered associations and complex multiple belongings.

The artworks featured in Hemmings' exhibition were bound together by the unravelling of interwoven, cross-cultural conversations and entangled histories, set in motion by historical and contemporary migrations. *Migrations* was indeed about the movement of peoples and objects, however Hemmings elegantly explored the fact that, "textiles are a place where multiple cultures come together"[21]. Thus every piece had not just one, but many stories to tell. There is so much more to a throwaway woven plastic holdall than first meets the eye.

Migrations
22 October - 21 January 2017

Curated by Professor Jessica Hemmings University of Gothenburg Sweden

Reviewed by Dr Christine Checinska University of Johannesburg

Two is the smallest unit of Being[22]

Discursive Documents highlights a productive tension in the capacity of a photographic image, both still and moving, to exist as a document and to hold discursive potential. The tension in between functioning as an aesthetic object, making reference to an object, and the ability of an image to unlock fictional subjectivities. The exhibition aims to test the social and political potential of 'discursive documents' to engender debate and social change – an optimistic, or even utopian, curatorial proposition.

The photograph continues to reinvent itself with the world wide web, digitally encoded and transmitted in the data stream more than it is a singular object held in the hand of the beholder. The seesaw state between these characteristics becomes ever more significant. As too is the discursive quality, all that it relates to beyond itself, and the discipline and decisions of photographer's practice. Ultimately, it seems, this exhibition broadly explores this inherent ontological bind within the medium and all that it touches.

There are many pairings at work in *Discursive Documents* besides the paradoxical title: the coming together of two public institutions to form ROTOЯ, and the three thematic propositions (the constructed feminine body, migration, and photography and the everyday) each comprising a pairing of artists. Also discernible in the images are the exchanges between photographer and subject (at times becoming tested[23]), between image and anticipated viewer, object and language, individual subjectivity and ideology.

We walk the space between works that are positioned left and right in conversation with one another. In these places and throughout the duration of the show are scheduled debates designed to question the (possibly utopian) possibilities of the work and bring us closer to the photographers, involved individuals and the context of the partnered institutions.

To the left, on entering, is a small, wall mounted Perspex box, lettered with a lover's poem. It contains the disembodied head, of a an inflatable 'sex-doll,' named Dolores by the artist, after she chanced upon the object for sale in a vending machine in China. Dolores, gazes blankly onto the deflating on-screen body, pink folds and teats slowly decompressing. Inflatable hands and feet are animated, seemingly moving of their own accord, to tuck back into a packaged, portable state. The left of her head, her dismembered parts are overlaid onto acetate hanging from the ceiling. This work, by Layla Sailor, corresponds to a Gif on the opposing wall, by Sarah Eyre, in which a circling collage of abstracted faces create moments of connection that resonate and either confirm or challenge our expectations of the forms contained within. If you walk behind the transparent hanging, as you are drawn to do, you view one work through the other, collaged body parts, still and moving, reforming to become an unreadable plastic mass; seduction undone.

Through cutting and splicing magazine images of the female form, Sarah Eyre re-appropriates the image of the female body and offers it beguilingly back to the viewer in a mismatched state that requires extra attention to navigate. Here the constructed artificiality of the 'original' is revealed, the object of desire has been reconfigured almost to the point of abstraction.

A kaleidoscopic orgy of meeting and parting lips and skin continually form and depart from what we recognize, as we search for what we know. The seductive power of the image endures, even as the work reveals the nonsense of the construction of femininity. Its construed elements move towards a reductive objectification, an alienation of the female self from the sum of her mismatched alluring parts, almost to the point of unreadability, and yet we still want it. We want our desire for the familiar to be rewarded, we crave completeness.

As we watch the sadly decompressing doll, her hands and feet lifting as they are exhausted of air, we connect to this emotionally. What we notice in ourselves, time and time again, is that whilst we knowingly adhere to the post empirical perspective on photography in theoretical terms, in actuality, we still want to believe that they represent a true reality. The persistence of the reality of a photograph becomes a fiction that we will knowingly accept.

In the next portion of the exhibition is a pairing concerned with the representation of migration, an unfolding conversation between Alex Baldea and Seba Kurtis, which further develops the curatorial proposition.

In Kurtis's portraits, layers and transparency are again at work. The colourful overworking in post-production distances and simultaneously brings us closer to the subject. Male faces are overlaid with dappled translucent planes and ambiguous sculptural forms, like rocks. This series was conceived around the story of a migrant travelling in a lorry of talc, the body overlaid in suffocating powder. As I move around the portraits, I notice that I am being watched from wherever I position myself; their gaze renders me the subject. I later learned that the work was also informed by reports of migrants attempting to pass a CO2 detector by

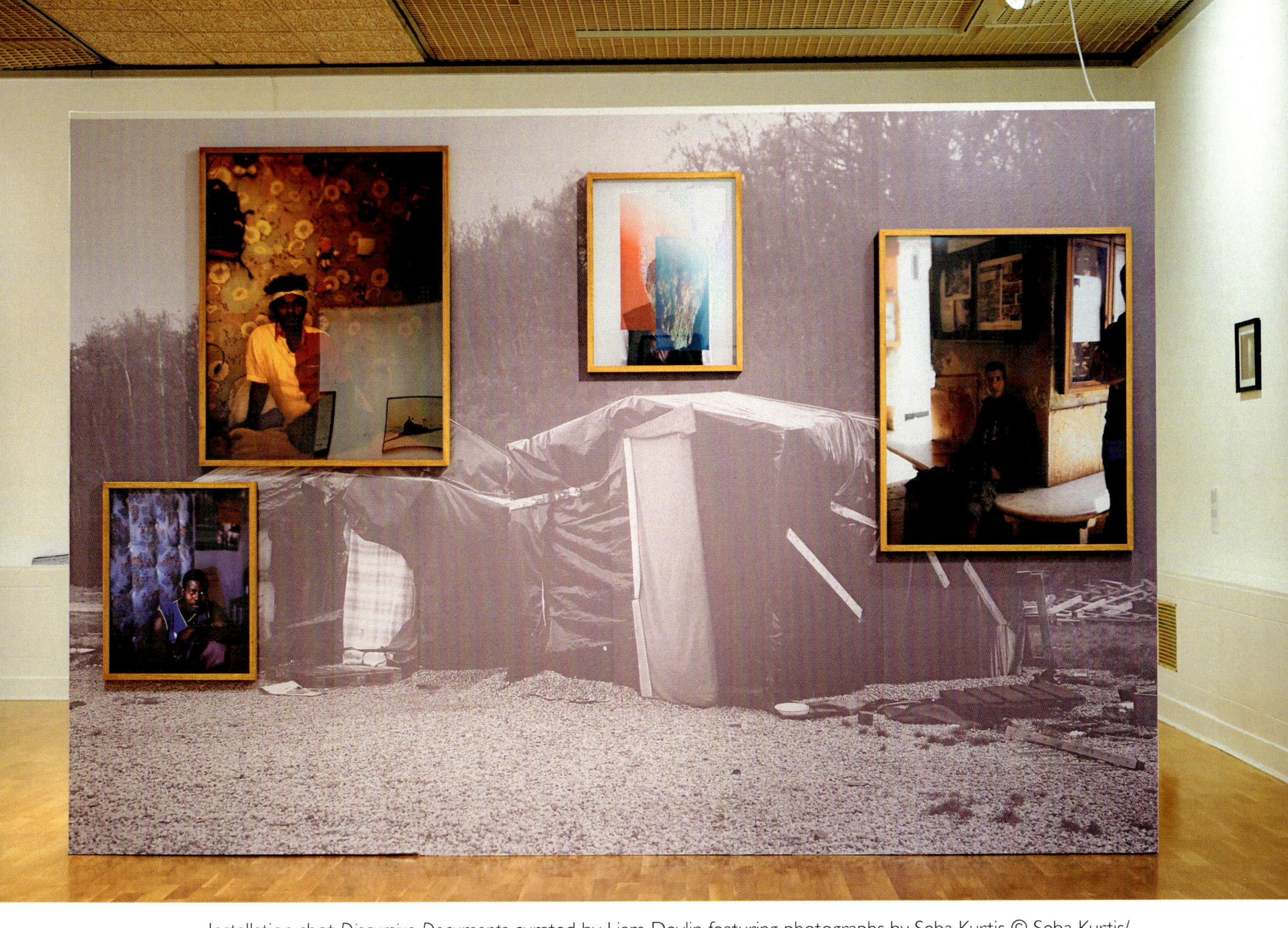

Installation shot *Discursive Documents* curated by Liam Devlin featuring photographs by Seba Kurtis © Seba Kurtis/ Courtesy of Christophe Guye Galerie

placing plastic bags over their heads. Many do not survive. The form I had mistaken for the surface of a rock, was a clear inflated bag to eliminate the presence of something living by the employed scanning technology.

Alex Baldea's work is assembled of images taken on migrant journeys across the channel; self-portraits on camera phones, documenting journeys and arrivals into unknown places. Representations of self-photographing selves invokes an uneasily everyday experience. Overhead is a large reproduced drawing of heads floating above water. This is paired with a self-published book and a video of found and recorded footage, an assembly of work made by Baldea and those featured.

Baldea's relationship with the migrants begins when they have arrived, but still await a destination, their status constantly one of transition and flux. In the construction of these images as documents, we see his voice in their journey and their voice in his work. The hierarchies at work in the presentation of these documents make it possible for all of this to become theoretically flawed. How can we make work, which references these structures, the ideologies that go into the construction and re-presentation of images? Speaking informally to Baldea, outside of the gallery space, went some way towards answering this question. His work does not represent the voice of migrants he has met, but is his subjective response to what he has witnessed. He works in opposition to material mediated through a network of capitalist mechanisms.

The final pairing opens up the theme of photography and the everyday as a relationship between public and private experience, internal and external worlds. To occupy the conversational space between Richard Higginbottom and Richard Mulhearn's delicately-pinned wall based prints and accompanying publications, is to move between these modes.

Richard Higginbottom's work *'Cut/Weld'* explores the city (Manchester) as a series of caught moments in which there is no beginning or end, only the continuity of an irregular rhythm and life beyond the frame. Consistent in their use of dramatic light and shade, *Cut/Weld* casts a net over a "swarming mass of immeasurable singularities"[24], pooling disparate elements and temporarily holding them together. His large wall based works cause us to pass passers by almost as if in the street, contrasting with the intimacy of the same images in book form.

In Richard Mulhearn's *'Kerb'*, the camera acts both as recorder and provocateur, revealing a collision between external and internal behaviours. They reveal unconscious moments of 'unbehaviour' – actions that don't fit, that exist beyond what is ideologically determined or expected. Three girls on a pavement are caught in a dissonant moment of captured contortion, chaotic zigzag limbs and face alarmingly lost to us in its unknowable expression. The back of an elderly woman as she stoops in a doorway, familiar but unexpected.

Higginbottom's newspaper[25] and Mulhearn's book provide opportunities for the encounter with their work to exist within the public space, but also travel outside of the institution. The authoritative voice of the institution and of the image as document is disrupted by intimacy. Between the wall-pinned prints and Higginbottom's unbound leaves, which have the potential to be reordered or discarded, the discursive nature of the documentary image takes precedent over its potential as evidence. What is more important is the exchange between photographer and viewer. The document diminishes and the intent of the photographer as mediator emerges more strongly.

On the closing night, at the end of speeches, I watched as a group of dancers animated the space. As the crowd spread to reveal where they had been quietly poised until now, they ran around the space interpreting and moving on, mirroring the visitors meandering between themes, digressing from subject to subject[26]. The dancers were not part of *Discursive Documents* per se, but rather an autonomous intervention for ROTOЯ. However, this occurrence was the only time that the exhibition transcended the pairings, to be interpreted as a whole, beyond duality to an interconnectivity of subjects and images. Coming to rest outside one image, the audience pausing with them, flowing bodies linked everything like a thread.

This event rendered the works an image stream as dancers moved from one to another, and our eyes followed them, perhaps similar to the way we might view such images outside of the gallery, in the urban environment or online. Eyes follow this thread, they look for similarities, the echo of our internal image bank as we navigate by familiarity, not difference. Viewers become a body and I am reminded that an exhibition is another way the image becomes part of a mediated environment, visitors passive recipients in the viewing process[27].

As opposed to a palette knife smoothing over, rendering everything the same, curator Liam Devlin's pairings heighten difference. In the programmed debates, differences emerge between seemingly similar works. Differences are revealed between the artists' intentions, the mechanisms behind the construction, and the possible ways to read of the images, the processes of imagining, editing, sequencing and display.

Presenting bodies of work more informally as process, with a fluidity between format works towards an acknowledgement of underlying authoritative structures. It brings us closer to the constructed nature of presentation which, in galleries, as well as online, is designed to influence behaviour, passage, interpretation and outcome.

The utopian act is one of pure revealing. In the conversational pairings and presentation of process, difference becomes the debate. It is this potential that is offered here for unveiling, unravelling, seeing and re-knowing - that which exists but has not previously been framed. Getting to the heart of the individual intention in the photographic moment that gives the image as document its strongest transformative possibility.

Photography offers a unique opportunity to get in between these cracks – in its ability to capture and record what cannot be ordinarily seen and therefore, known. The problem lies in making the unseeable seen. Once captured, owned and presented, the subjective act becomes broken, implicated in ideology, and so, the camera becomes its accomplice.

Photography requires ideology in order to function – it requires myth. When we try to break it, the power of the photographic document dissolves, and is then resumed by our compulsive desire for it. The document is born of a fictional act. Sometimes it captures something unexpected and it is in the process of editing or sequencing that the intention is revealed, through narrative in the mind of the photographer. The moment of making is to anticipate the future and turn it into the past, to first act discursively, and then to create a document. Photography is first conceived in and of language. It then becomes a document in taking up a physical or shareable form – it then functions again as language. The 'discursive document' whilst operating under the strain of its (theoretical) productive tension, is less of a contradiction in reality as it is according to our lingering empirical bias. Photography, like us, in its existential dualism cannot be understood in any smaller way.

Discursive Documents
11 February - 4 May 2017

Curated by Dr Liam Devlin University of Huddersfield

Reviewed by Anna Taylor

Notes and citations

1 Hemmings, J., (2015) *Cultural Threads: transnational textiles today.* London: Bloomsbury

2 See the childrensartschool.co.uk.

3 See funpalaces.co.uk.

4 Huddersfield Contemporary Music Festival was founded in 1978, early participants include John Cage, Karlheinz Stockhausen, Brian Eno and many other major figures on the contemporary music and improvisation scene.

5 The Gannex company supplied Harold Wilson with his signature waterproof raincoat in the 1960s.

6 Designed by the architect James Pigott Pritchett and built by the firm of Joseph Kaye in 1846-50 using the neo-classical style, John Betjemin later described it as one of the most splendid station façades in England, second only to St. Pancras, London. See http://openbuildings.com/buildings/huddersfield-railway-station-profile-10274

7 http://heritagequay.org/huddersfieldgems/huddersfieldcentrallibrary/
Opened in 1940, designed by architect Edward H. Ashburner, the building utised local Crosland Moor stone was used to face the building. The Art Gallery opened in 1943.

8 Poetic thought position #70/500 composed by a generative process on 15th October 2015 by Rob Lycett see www.breakingthings.info

9 Poetic thought position #69/500 composed by a generative process on 15th October 2015 by Rob Lycett see www.breakingthings.info

10 These quotes on the posters were subsequently posted on Twitter.

11 Sheila Gaffney, Reflections on the Good, the Bad and the Ugly, https://www.hud.ac.uk/research/researchcentres/st/thoughtpositionsinsculpture/sheilagaffney/

12 I interviewed Rosemary Butler at length 1999-2000 for the British Library National Life Stories Artists' Lives project, reference C466/94. See www.bl.uk

13 Juliet MacDonald, Displaying the Head of Victory, https://www.hud.ac.uk/research/researchcentres/st/thoughtpositionsinsculpture/julietmacdonald/

14 See Note 12. Other artists I interviewed for the British Library National Life Stories Artists' Lives project include Bruce Lacey, Ralph Brown, Pat Whitehead and Jacqueline Morreau.

15 Hester Reeve, The artist lives, long live the artist!, https://www.hud.ac.uk/research/researchcentres/st/thoughtpositionsinsculpture/hesterreeve/

16 Den Hartog, H. (2010) *Shanghai New Towns: Searching for Community and Identity in a Sprawling Metropolis.* Rotterdam: 010 Publishers.

17 Chen, Y.; Zheng, S. (2010). *The Buildings of World Exposition.* Shanghai: Shanghai University Press.

18 Hemmings, J. (2016), *Migrations*, Hudderfield Art Gallery, exhibition video.

19 Anatsui, E. (2003), cited *The Essential Art of African Textiles*: Design Without End http://www.metmuseum.org/exhibitions/listings/2008/african-textiles/el-anatsui

20 Kaur, J. in Hemmings J, (2105), *Cultural Threads: Transnational Textiles Today,* Bloomsbury Publications: London, p. 18.

21 Hemmings, J. (2016), *Migrations*, Hudderfield Art Gallery, exhibition video.

22 "It is also only through this interlocking that we ourselves exist. Two is the smallest unit of Being." Kaja Silverman, The Miracle of Analogy or The History of Photography, Part 1 (Stanford University Press) 2015

23 For example, in Baldea's re-appropriated images taken as the self-documentation of the subject

24 de Certeau, M. (1984) *Walking in the City, in The Practice of Everyday Life.* Berkeley: University of California Press

25 Both produced by Tide Press, 2017

26 The Latin verb "discurrere" meant "to run about", from which we get our word discursive.

27 Reference to Adorno and Horkheimer (2007, originally published 1944), *The Dialectic of Enlightenment.* Verso Classics

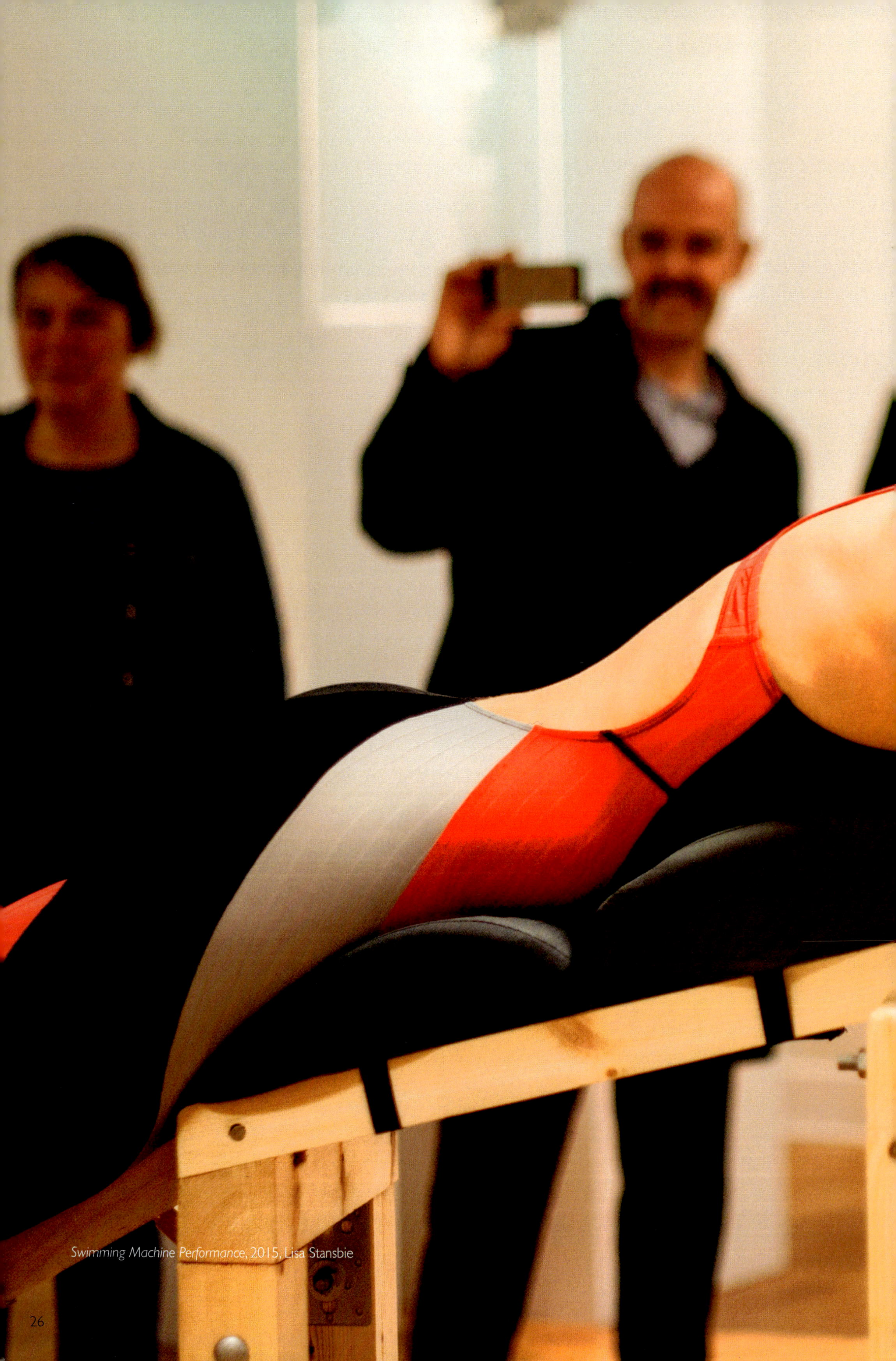

Swimming Machine Performance, 2015, Lisa Stansbie